OSPREY COMBAT AIRCRAFT • 29

MiG-21
UNITS OF THE
VIETNAM WAR

SERIES EDITOR: TONY HOLMES

OSPREY COMBAT AIRCRAFT • 29

MiG-21 UNITS OF THE VIETNAM WAR

István Toperczer

OSPREY
PUBLISHING

Front Cover
On 27 April 1972, a pair of US Navy F-4B Phantom IIs from VF-51 launched from the aircraft carrier USS *Coral Sea* (CVA-43) and headed in the direction of Hanoi. One of the jets (BuNo 153025) was flown by Lt Albert R Molinare, with Lt Cdr James B Souder as his Radar Intercept Officer (RIO). Both Phantom IIs were armed with AIM-9 Sidewinder and AIM-7 Sparrow air-to-air missiles, as well as cluster bomb units.

En route to the target, the crews indulged in a spot of ground-strafing when they caught a truck heading north on Highway 1. Upon reaching their designated patrol area, which was about 90 miles south of Hanoi, the F-4s maintained station just west of the target area. At the same time, the 921st 'Sao Do' Fighter Regiment's Hoang Quoc Dung and Cao Son Khao took off from Noi Bai air base in their MiG-21s. Within minutes of launching, both pilots spotted the two F-4Bs some six kilometres ahead of them.

Having closed the separation distance to just three kilometres, Hoang Quoc Dung fired an R-3S (K-13 Atoll) air-to-air missile at the Phantom II flown by Molinare and Souder. Seconds later the VF-51 jet was hit, and it immediately burst into flames and crashed near Vu Ban. The crew successfully ejected and were captured upon reaching the ground – they were held as prisoners of war in the infamous 'Hanoi Hilton' jail until their release in March 1973. James Souder subsequently calculated that he had spent one day in prison for each mission he had flown between November 1971 and when he was shot down.

Almost five years earlier, on 26 October 1967, Souder had led a pair of F-4Bs from VF-143 (off the USS *Constellation*) in an interception against a North Vietnamese MiG-21 flown by Mai Van Cuong. Closing on the MiG, Souder's pilot was unable to fire his missiles due to a technical fault, so he ordered his wingman (Lt(jg) Robert P Hickey Jr, with Lt(jg) Jeremy G Morris as his RIO, in F-4B BuNo 149411) to shoot. The MiG was brought down with a single AIM-7 Sparrow missile just south of Hanoi. That was the same mission on which future Republican Presidential nominee Lt Cdr John S McCain of

Dedication
For Nguyen Van Coc and Pham Tuan

First published in Great Britain in 2001 by Osprey Publishing
Elms Court, Chapel Way, Botley, Oxford, OX2 9LP

ISBN 1 84176 263 6

Edited by Tony Holmes, Neil Maxwell and Peter Mersky
Page design by Tony Truscott
Cover Artwork by Iain Wyllie
Aircraft Profiles and Scale Drawings by Mark Styling
Origination by Grasmere Digital Imaging, Leeds, UK
Printed in Hong Kong through Bookbuilders

00 01 02 03 04   10 9 8 7 6 5 4 3 2 1

EDITOR'S NOTE
To make this best-selling series as authoritative as possible, the Editor would be interested in hearing from any individual who may have relevant photographs, documentation or first-hand experiences relating to the world's combat aircraft, and the crews that flew them, in the various theatres of war. Any material used will be credited to its original source. Please write to Tony Holmes at 10 Prospect Road, Sevenoaks, Kent, TN13 3UA, Great Britain, or by e-mail at: tony.holmes@osprey-jets.freeserve.co.uk

ACKNOWLEDGEMENTS
I would like to thank the following individuals and organisations for their help and support – John D Sherwood, Thomas J Hanton, W Howard Plunkett, James B Souder, William H Talley, Charles N Tanner, Nguyen Van Coc, Nguyen Van Dinh, Dao Hoang Giang, Trung H Huynh, Tran Dinh Kiem, Truong Van Minh, Nguyen Viet Phuc, Pham Tuan, Jósef Beke, Ernö Bohar, Dr Miklós Déri, Gábor Pálfai, Zoltán Pintér, Gábor Szekeres, the museums of the Vietnamese People's Air Force, the Embassy of the Socialist Republic of Vietnam in Budapest, the Embassy of Hungary in Hanoi, and the Ministry of Foreign Affairs of the Socialist Republic of Vietnam in Hanoi.

VA-163 (off the USS *Oriskany*) found himself parachuting into Truch Bach lake in Hanoi after his A-4E Skyhawk (BuNo 149959) was struck by an SA-2 surface-to-air missile (*Cover artwork by Iain Wyllie*)

Back Cover
Two 'Fishbed' pilots stroll past a pair of MiG-21MFs and a two-seat MiG-21U of the 927th Fighter Regiment as they undergo routine maintenance (*Tran Dinh Kiem Collection*)

CONTENTS

BEYOND MACH 2.0

From July 1965, batteries of North Vietnamese SA-2 surface-to-air missiles started to enter service, operated by Soviet experts. These missiles were highly effective, and in order to counter their threat, American pilots were forced to fly at lower altitudes. This in turn made them susceptible to attack by the handful of MiG-17 fighters that then equipped the Vietnamese People's Air Force (VPAF).

From the end of that year, the conflict between the American and North Vietnamese air forces dramatically increased in intensity following the introduction of the first MiG-21F-13 'Fishbed-Cs', which boasted air-to-air missile capability. These had arrived in-theatre directly from the Soviet Union, and in April 1966 the VPAF introduced its first MiG-21PF 'Fishbed-D' interceptors.

The unit chosen to debut the 'Fishbed' in combat was the VPAF's oldest fighter regiment, the 921st 'Sao Do'. A handful of its pilots, including future ranking aces Nguyen Van Coc, Pham Thanh Ngan and Nguyen Hong Nhi, had already trained on MiG-21s in the Soviet Union,

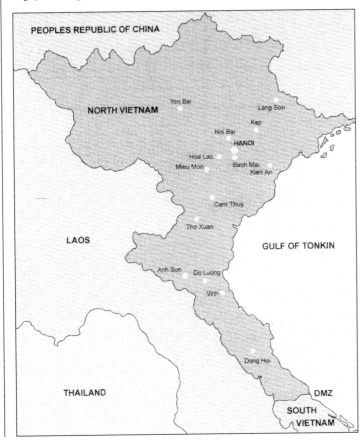

PEOPLES REPUBLIC OF CHINA

NORTH VIETNAM

Yen Bai
Lang Son
Kep
Noi Bai
HANOI
Hoa Lac
Mieu Mon
Bach Mai
Kien An
Cam Thuy
Tho Xuan
LAOS
GULF OF TONKIN
Anh Son
Do Luong
Vinh
Dong Hoi
THAILAND
DMZ
SOUTH VIETNAM

This map reveals the location of all the major airfields from which the VPAF operated MiG-21s during the conflict in Vietnam

The VPAF received its first MiG-21F-13 'Fishbed-Cs' from the USSR in late 1965, and issued them to its most experienced fighter regiment, the 921st 'Sao Do' at Noi Bai (*VNA*)

CO of the 921st, Tran Hanh (left) briefs young pilots at Noi Bai in 1966. All of them are wearing the tight-fitting green high-altitude flying suits synonymous with 'Fishbed' operations in the early years of the war. The pilots' personal equipment is completed by a bulky GS-4 helmet – a far cry from the SL-60 leather helmet that they would have worn when flying the MiG-15UTI and JJ-5 during conversion training! Two MiG-21PF 'Fishbed-Ds' of the 921st 'Sao Do' can be seen parked in the background (*Truong Van Minh*)

and now Pham Ngoc Lan, Nguyen Ngoc Do and Nguyen Nhat Chieu were also chosen for conversion onto the type. Dao Dinh Luyen and Tran Hanh (the latter pilot took command of the 921st in 1966) also took part in the conversion programme.

In the USSR, L-29s and MiG-21Us had been used to prepare the pilots for the 'Fishbed', but these types were not available in Vietnam, so the VPAF initially made do with MiG-15UTIs. Chinese-built Shenyang JJ-5 two-seaters (derived from the MiG-17) were also subsequently used.

By late January 1966, the 921st Fighter Regiment felt confident enough to commence operational flying, and the MiG-21F-13s were duly introduced to active service. Within a month the type was fighting alongside the regiment's venerable MiG-17s.

MiG-21 pilots initially got accustomed to 'combat' by intercepting American Ryan Firebee unmanned reconnaissance drones, the first of these being downed on 4 March 1966. At 0400 hrs on this date, Vietnamese radar units reported an unmanned reconnaissance aircraft intruding from the north-east. The 921st Fighter Regiment's deputy commander, Tran Hanh, ordered Nguyen Hong Nhi to take off, and 19 minutes later he reported that he was at an altitude of 16,000 m, and that his target was still 15 kilometres away and 2000 m above him, flying towards Quang Ninh. Ground controllers ordered him to close in and attack, and within minutes the regiment had chalked up its first 'kill'. A second drone was destroyed the following day.

Both Firebees had been attacked at an altitude of about 18,000 m, some 70 kilometres north of Hanoi. The MiG pilots had destroyed the drones with single Atoll AAMs, fired at distances of between two and four kilometres. These were the first US reconnaissance drones to be brought down by the VPAF.

The following month the MiG-21s at last engaged manned aircraft, but on this occasion victory eluded them. The first combat took place on 23 April, when two 'Fishbeds' attacked a flight of F-4s. Despite flying their fighters to the best of their ability, the communist pilots were unable to fire their R-3S missiles because they could not achieve a positive radar lock. Three more engagements in April and May saw no less than 14 AAMs fired, but not one hit its target. Losses were also suffered when several VPAF pilots ran out of fuel and were forced to eject after lengthy engagements with the enemy. And a solitary MiG-21 was shot down by an F-4C crew (from the 480th TFS/35th TFW) on 26 April.

When the VPAF analysed the dogfights of April and May, it became apparent that pilots were struggling to come to terms with the radar system fitted in the MiG-21. When searching for a target, the pilot would use radar, and once the target had been located, he would close in on his prey and switch to an optical sighting system before firing. And this was when the problems started.

The pilot of the target aircraft would be doing everything possible to shake off his pursuer, while the Vietnamese attacker would be desperately trying to keep the target in his sights sufficiently long enough to judge its range, before deciding whether to fire a missile. Flying the fighter while effectively working the radar and optical sight was a skill that could only be acquired through experience, which the Vietnamese MiG-21 pilots were glaringly short of in the spring of 1966.

The VPAF also found that 'Fishbeds' operating in pairs were

An instructor and his student discuss the take-off characteristics of the MiG-21 in one of the numerous classrooms utilised by the 921st Fighter Regiment at Noi Bai

On 4 and 5 March 1966, MiG-21s from the 921st used R-3S (dubbed the K-13 Atoll by the Americans) AAMs to shoot down two Ryan Firebee umanned photo-reconnaissance drones that were overflying North Vietnam at high altitude. The wreckage of these craft was placed on display in Hanoi (*Gábor Pálfai*)

more successful when they went into combat armed with a mix of weapons. A typical mission fit would see the lead pilot's aircraft armed with two infra-red guided R-3S AAMs, while his wingman's MiG-21 would boast two UB-16-57 pods loaded with S-5M unguided rockets.

And it was with this weapons load that a pair of MiG-21PF 'Fishbed-Ds' attacked two F-105s at an altitude of just 500 m on 7 June 1966. The trailing MiG opened fire from 1500 m, but the Thunderchief initially evaded the fusilade of unguided rockets by making an evasive left turn. Undeterred, the communist pilot pressed home his attack, firing two more salvoes of missiles from 500 and 200 m, which reportedly destroyed the F-105 – official USAF loss records fail to confirm this claim, however.

In the meantime, the flight leader was unable to lock his R-3S onto the second F-105 due to the USAF pilot's frantic manoeuvring, and in the end the Vietnamese pilot did not fire. Two similar dogfights that took place just days later provided further evidence that the VPAF pilots could have been more successful if their jets had been equipped with cannon. At this stage in the war, MiG-21PF 'Fishbed-Ds' delivered to Vietnam were provided without the optional centreline GP-9 cannon pod.

Rules for MiG-21 pilots engaging a foe were clearly laid out. Aircraft were only scrambled on the direct orders of central command, and only when an attack was imminent could a fighter regiment's commander order aircraft on stand-by alert to take off. This strict military doctrine confined the pilots to a dogfighting role, instead of playing to the MiG-21's clear strength as a high-speed interceptor. These rules undoubtedly prevented the VPAF from achieving early successes.

Senior officers in Hanoi also stipulated that aircraft flying in pairs would remain between 50 and 200 m apart. In flights of four, each pair would maintain a distance of between 300 and 700 m from the other. However, this was later modified to 500-800 m and 800 m respectively, as it was found that a widely spread formation presented intercepting US fighters with a more difficult target. Such open formations only became possible after the 'Fishbeds' began operating above altitudes of 2500 m.

In an effort to make the MiG-21 more manoeuvrable, a choice was also made in favour of the R-3S missile instead of the unguided S-5M carried in bulky UB-16-57 pods.

By June 1966, an additional 13 pilots had completed their training in the Soviet Union, and on the 9th of the month two MiG-21s from the 921st Fighter Regiment claimed two Phantom IIs destroyed with missiles – again US loss records do not list any jets downed by MiG activity.

During 1966 the combat effectiveness of the VPAF improved considerably, with the MiG-17 force in particular beginning to inflict sustained losses on US aircraft. However, the same could not be said for the MiG-21-equipped 921st, for despite participating in several dogfights, the regiment failed to down any aircraft. Meetings were held to discuss the problem, and it was decided that 'Fishbed' pilots were less successful because they were not yet fully familiar with their aircraft, and that most of them were still using tactics that had been drummed into them when they were flying the MiG-17.

Things only began to change when senior officers studied the pattern of American attacks, which in turn prompted the revision of interception techniques. These new tactics called for MiG-17s and -21s to jointly conduct combat air patrols (CAPs) in airspace most often used by incoming US fighter-bombers. The MiG-17s would patrol at a low altitude (up to 1500 m), while the MiG-21s from the 921st's base at Noi Bai would fly above them (at altitudes in excess of 2500 m). Anywhere between 1500 and 2500 m was considered to be an intermediate zone where both types could take part in dogfights.

VPAF pilots enjoyed one distinct advantage over their US counterparts, for they were more familiar with the local terrain, including the mountains, and had good support from ground control units.

On 7 July, Vietnamese radar picked up a number of US aircraft approaching from Thailand. Two MiG-21s, piloted by Nguyen Nhat Chieu and Tran Ngoc Xiu, were scrambled from Noi Bai and ordered to remain on CAP over the area. When the F-105Ds appeared from behind Tam Dao mountain, Tran Ngoc Xiu attacked with AAMs, shooting down one of the intruders – no USAF losses were recorded on this day. On the 11th, Vu Ngoc Dinh and Dong Van Song downed another F-105D (61-0121 of the 355th TFW, flown by Maj W L McClelland) over Son Duong, in Tuyen Quang province. The USAF claimed that the jet was lost through fuel exhaustion after an engagement with a MiG-21.

The Americans swiftly exacted their revenge, however, claiming two MiG-21s destroyed on 14 July by F-4Cs from the 480th TFS/35th TFW.

Numerous aerial engagements took place during the second half of 1966 involving MiG-21s. One such action took place on 21 September, when patrolling 'Fishbeds' detected a formation of F-4s and F-105s. The lead MiG-21 pilot attacked a Thunderchief, and later claimed it shot down with an R-3S missile fired from a distance of 1500 m. The weapon was launched at the limit of the targeting system's operational envelope, at a height of 1200 m and a speed of 700 km/h – the USAF admitted the loss of an F-105D, but credited its destruction to a SAM.

On 5 October the air force also recorded the destruction of F-4C 64-0702 of the 433rd TFS/8th TFW by a MiG-21, although on this occasion there was no corresponding claim by the VPAF.

Three days later the VPAF's MiG-21 force celebrated its first US Navy kill when two Phantom IIs were claimed to have been destroyed by AAMs. One of those aircraft was F-4B BuNo 152093 of VF-154, crewed by Lt Cdr Charles Tanner (pilot) and Lt Ross R Terry (RIO). In the following account, Tanner vividly remembers that day, and the events that were to follow;

'I was flying an F-4B off the USS *Coral Sea*. Lt Ross Terry was flying as my RIO. Our mission was two-fold. As the lead of a flight of four F-4Bs that were part of a larger bomb group made up of A-4s, we had two jobs. First, we were to suppress flak by dropping 500-lb bombs on active AAA in the target area, and then we were to cover the A-4s leaving the target as TARCAP (Target Combat Air Patrol).

Nguyen Van Minh (left) demonstrates how he 'shot down' F-4B Phantom II BuNo 152093 of VF-154 on 9 October 1966. The crew of the USS *Coral Sea*-based fighter were captured and subsequently tortured to admit that they had been downed by an AAM fired from a MiG-21. However, upon their release in 1973, the naval aviators stated that their fighter had almost certainly been struck by AAA, and this is how the loss is recorded in official US Navy records (*Truong Van Minh*)

'We were closing on the target – the Phu Ly railyard – and I estimated it was less than 20 seconds prior to roll-in at 14,000 ft/500 knots. We were leading all the elements, as our target was the AAA guns located in the yard. We had accelerated ahead of the A-4 flight to be off target when they rolled in on the railyard. My wingman was behind me, and spread. He was not hit by any fire. Having varied our altitude and heading until the last 30 seconds, we then levelled out to make sure we had good visual contact with the target.

'It was then that a sharp explosion beneath the aircraft took out all electrical power and all but one hydraulic system. The engines were still producing full thrust, so we broke hard right to break loose of whatever weapon system had locked on. Gradually, the hydraulics went, the throttles had no control of the engines, and we rolled into about a 135° bank with a 60° nose-down angle. Our speed was mach 1.3 when I ejected.

'Ross and I were captured and imprisoned until repatriation $6^{1}/_{2}$ years later. The imprisonment began with physical torture to try to obtain military information, as well as derive propaganda value from our capture. They tried to get Ross and I to say we were shot down by a MiG-21. After about eight hours of continuous torture, Ross told his interrogators that he had been shot down by a MiG. The story about being shot by a MiG was apparently what they wanted to hear because the beatings stopped immediately.'

The VF-154 jet was the only F-4 lost on 9 October, and its demise was almost certainly brought about by a well-aimed burst of flak, rather than an AAM. That same day the Navy claimed its first MiG-21 kill when VF-162's CO, Cdr Dick Bellinger, downed a 'Fishbed' with a Sidewinder whilst flying an F-8E off the USS *Oriskany* (CVA-34). The USAF struck again on 5 November when the destruction of two MiG-21s was credited to a pair of F-4Cs from the 480th TFS/366th TFW.

More clashes took place in early December, with the first encounters taking place on the 2nd when the airfield at Noi Bai became the focus of attention for F-4s and F-105s. Three pairs of MiG-21s were scrambled to defend the base, and the leader of the first flight launched an R-3S at a Phantom II from 1200-1500 m and claimed a kill. With his wingman unable to fire his UB rocket pods due to his target being too far away, the leader in turn shot off his remaining missile at another formation of F-4s, but the R-3S, launched from a distance of four kilometres, missed.

The leader of the second flight also added a Phantom II to the list of victories claimed on this day, but by the time the third flight arrived on the scene, the departing jets were out of range, and their missiles failed to find a target. The USAF recorded the loss of two F-4Cs on 2 December, but once again attributed their destruction to SAMs.

Up until the end of 1966, the VPAF's tactics meant that its fighters

Nguyen Ngoc Xiu (centre) and Dong Van De (left) claimed two Thunderchiefs destroyed on 14 December 1966, although US sources only note the loss of Capt Robert Cooley's F-105D (60-0502 of the 357th TFS/355th TFW) (*Truong Van Minh*)

As previously mentioned, Tran Hanh was the commander of the 921st in 1966, having been one of the first VPAF pilots to participate in the conversion programme that saw a number of the regiment's more experienced MiG-17 pilots transition onto the MiG-21. He had been credited with two kills flying the 'Fresco' in 1965, prior to becoming a 'Fishbed' pilot (*Tran Dinh Kiem*)

This pathetic pile of charred and twisted metal was all that remained of Capt Robert Cooley's F-105D after it had been shot down by an AAM on 14 December 1966. Although the VNAF had claimed over a dozen victories with the MiG-21/R-3S combination by this stage of the war, Cooley's jet was the first to be officially recognised by the USAF as having been downed by an AAM (*VNA*)

remained in the vicinity of their own airfield, and intercepted only when American aircraft intruded into their particular airspace. However, Russian advisors recommended that intercept areas be moved away from the intended target, and this meant that a US strike force would still be in close formation when VPAF aircraft found it, and its aircraft would be easier to hit. Just such an engagement took place on 5 December.

Two pairs of MiG-21s had been scrambled from Noi Bai, the pilots being told to head for an area some 35 kilometres away. Twenty-four American aircraft – a mixture of F-4s and F-105s – were flying through the region in a long formation, with between one and two minutes separating the flights. The first pair of MiGs attacked the lead flight and hit a Thunderchief, while the second pair attacked the next flight, bringing down another F-105. The Americans turned round and headed for home. The USAF recorded the loss of a single F-105D (62-4331 of the 421st TFS/388th TFW), its pilot, Maj B N Begley, being posted Missing in Action (MIA). The air force also noted that the F-105 had been downed by a 'MiG-17'.

Three days later, the intercept zone was moved 50 kilometres away from Noi Bai, and once again two pairs of MiG-21s managed to claim two F-105s – the USAF admitted no losses to MiGs on this day. Finally, on 14 December, 20 F-105s were attacked by four MiG-21s, and the VPAF claimed to have destroyed three aircraft. The USAF credit the destruction of F-105D 60-0502 of the 357th TFS/355th TFW, flown by Capt R B Cooley (who was rescued), to an AAM fired by a MiG-21.

In the course of aerial engagements during December, the Vietnamese pilots came to believe in the capabilities of the R-3S missile, but only in cases where they were taking their target by surprise. To achieve this, they first had to mount a visual-only search for an enemy aircraft, and once they had located the intruder, they had to stay in its radar 'blind-spot'.

Most of the time, missiles would be launched from a distance of about 1200-2500 m – Soviet instructors thought a distance of 1500 m was best. Straight after firing, the Vietnamese pilot would roll away and remain at low level all the way back to base.

But the hunter would often become the hunted, and due to the 'Fishbed's' heavily framed canopy, detecting an AIM-9 Sidewinder being

launched was much more difficult for MiG-21 pilots than for those flying MiG-17s. It was the job of the MiG-21 wingman to watch his back, and that of his flight leader, and if he spotted a missile closing on either of them he would yell out a warning so they could perform a high-g turn into and below the round. This manoeuvre would usually break the lock of the AIM-9's infrared seeker head on the MiG-21's tailpipe. If the pilots performed this turn quickly enough, they would be able to dodge the missile, and live to fight another day.

VICTORIES AND LOSSES

The new year started badly for the VPAF, with no fewer than five MiG-21s being lost in just a matter of minutes over Noi Bai on 2 January 1967. All of these aircraft had fallen victim to F-4Cs of the 8th TFW, which was led by legendary World War 2 ace Col Robin Olds. This one-sided action had highlighted a major flaw in the VPAF's MiG-21 combat strategy, and although all the pilots (including future aces Vu Ngoc Dinh and Nguyen Van Coc) managed to eject, the loss of five aircraft (the USAF crews actually claimed seven kills) severely affected the morale of the 921st Fighter Regiment.

On this fateful day, Noi Bai's MiGs, and those at nearby Kep, had been placed on category one red alert after American intruders had been detected. The two airfields were blanketed in 10/10ths cloud, which started at a height of 1500 m and cleared at 3000 m.

Problems for the communist pilots started when central command, in Hanoi, forbade the MiGs from taking off until the US jets were just 40 kilometres from Noi Bai. However, by that time two additional flights of F-4Cs (from the 8th TFW) had flown into the area undetected, and were patrolling directly above the clouds overhead the airfield. Radarless MiG-17s were restricted to flying beneath the cloud base, and had therefore failed to detect the presence of enemy fighters.

One by one the MiG-21s took off, and one by one the first four were shot down by the waiting Phantom IIs. The same fate also befell the leader of the second 'Fishbed' formation to launch.

The losses were blamed on the late take-off of the 'alert' aircraft, as well as the indecisiveness of central command. Additionally, the tactics employed by the VPAF pilots once they were aloft were also badly flawed, for they should have broken through the cloud a clear distance away from the base, joined up, and then come back and attacked the waiting F-4s. Four days later the VPAF lost two more MiG-21s again to F-4Cs from the 8th TFW. One pilot ejected but the other was killed.

On 8 January, the VPAF's high command met to discuss what had gone wrong. New tactics were devised, which would see attacks performed guerrilla-style, with a quick strike and a quick retreat. Small groups of between two and four aircraft would be involved, with a maximum of ten in each mission. The altitude and speed of the attackers would also be constantly changed. Finally, after closely studying US tactics, VPAF commanders decided that MiG-21 pilots should attack the enemy from above, while those flying the MiG-17 would strike from either side. The implementation of these tactics would have to wait awhile, however, as the badly mauled 921st was withdrawn from combat for several months in order to make good its losses.

The USAF next encountered 'Fishbeds' on 23 April 1967, when an F-4C crew (this time from the 389th TFS/366th TFW) claimed a single MiG-21 destroyed. Five days later the air force attributed the loss of F-105D 58-1151 (of the 44th TFS/388th TFW) to a MiG-21, its pilot, Capt F A Caras, being listed as MIA. No VPAF claims were made on this date, however.

The new tactics implemented by the VPAF finally paid off on the last day of April, and once again the Thunderchief bore the brunt of the MiG-21 attacks. Radar units had detected American aircraft heading towards Vinh Phu, and the 921st was ordered to send up two flights of two MiG-21s. Future ranking VPAF ace Nguyen Van Coc remembers:

'I was scrambled as wingman to Nguyen Ngoc Do. I noticed F-105s flying beneath us at an altitude of 2500 m, at 30° to our course. My leader also saw the Thunderchiefs. We both increased our speed and dived at the US fighter-bombers, which were unaware of our presence. The leader shot down the second aeroplane in a group of four F-105s. Until now, I had been protecting my leader, but with an enemy fighter filling my sights, I also opened fire, downing another Thunderchief. We received an order to return to base and made a successful landing, while the eight F-105s dropped their bombs and started a search for the lost pilots.'

Squadronmates Le Trong Huyen and Vu Ngoc Dinh also enjoyed success during this mission, claiming two more F-105s destroyed. The USAF recorded the loss of two F-105Ds from the 355th TFW (59-1726 of the 354th TFS and 61-0130 of the 333rd TFS), flown by 1Lt R A Abbott and Capt J S Abbott, and a single F-105F (62-4447 of the 357th TFS/355th TFW), crewed by Maj L E Thorsness and Capt H E Johnson – all four men were captured. Eleven days earlier, Thorsness and Johnson had claimed a MiG-17 destroyed.

In May the Americans renewed their attacks on Hanoi, and the VPAF responded with up to 40 sorties each day. After losing a MiG-21 to Col Robin Olds (in a 555th TFS/8th TFW F-4C) on the 4th, the 921st struck back eight days later when Le Trong Huyen and Dong Van Song claimed an F-105F shot down over Van Yen, in Nghia Lo province – the USAF again listed this aircraft as having been downed by a SAM.

Two more 'Fishbeds' were claimed destroyed by F-4Cs from the 389th TFS/366th TFW on 20 May, and 48 hours later a further pair were credited to the CO of the 389th, Lt Col Robert F Titus. Flying with his Weapons System

Ho Chi Minh congratulates Capt Nguyen Van Coc on his first aerial victory on 30 April 1967. The MiG-21 pilot would score a further eight kills (*Tran Dinh Kiem*)

Two MiG-21s from the 921st (and a flight of MiG-17s) attacked twelve A-4s and four F-8s over Hai Duong on 11 July 1967. This Skyhawk was 'downed' by Le Trong Huyen, although the Navy claimed that no A-4s were lost on this day (*VNA*)

Pham Thanh Ngan (left) was credited with eight kills, while Nguyen Van Coc (right) shot down nine aircraft during the war. Here, they are seen wearing orange life-vests over their flying suits. The aces are flanking their commanding officer, Maj Tran Hanh (*VPAF Museum*)

Six-kill ace Nguyen Ngoc Do claimed his first victory on 30 April 1967, when he downed F-105D 59-1726 of the 354th TFS/355th TFW over Vinh Phu. He would go on to claim a further five kills by the end of 1968 (*VPAF Museum*)

Operator (WSO), 1Lt Milan Zimer, Titus had also downed one of the 'Fishbeds' destroyed on the 20th. A solitary F-4C had in turn been claimed over Hanoi by future seven-kill ace Dang Ngoc Ngu, although USAF records list this as a SAM shoot-down.

On 11 July, an American strike on the bridges at Lai Vu and Phu Luong, along Route 5, was met with stiff resistance from MiG-21s flown by Le Trong Huyen and Dong Van Song, in co-ordination with a flight of MiG-17s. The Vietnamese pilots bounced a group of twelve A-4s and four F-8s over Hai Duong, and one A-4 was claimed to have been destroyed – no Skyhawks were reportedly lost by the Navy on this day.

Six days later a flight of MiG-21s, with Nguyen Nhat Chieu in command, claimed an F-8 destroyed over Lang Chanh, in Thanh Hoa province. This was followed up on the 20th by the destruction of an F-4 Phantom II over Nho Quan, in Ninh Binh province, the kill being credited to Nguyen Ngoc Do and Pham Thanh Ngan. Once again, no such losses are included within official US records.

And although the two RF-4Cs claimed by the 921st on 26 July and 10 August do feature in USAF loss listings, these were credited to SAMs!

Recce Phantom II overflights of the north had become a routine occurrence by mid-1967, although the MiG-21 force had been unable to do anything about them until now. The first jet downed on 26 July had been flying the standard route followed by USAF photo-recce aircraft preparing to head back south when it had been spotted by a pair of MiG-21PF 'Fishbed-Ds'.

The MiG pilot reported that he had a visual fix on the intruder, who was between eight and ten kilometres ahead of him, cruising at an altitude of 5000 m. Going for afterburner, he closed on the Phantom II, which also increased its speed to 1200 km/h and began to descend. Reaching 1400 km/h, and an altitude of 3000 m, the MiG-21 launched an R-3S missile from a distance of three kilometres. The Phantom II was seen to be destroyed. The same fate befell the second RF-4C on 10 August.

This date had also seen Navy F-4s at last claim their first MiG-21 kills, when two VF-142 jets on a TARCAP sortie from the *Constellation* bagged a pair of 'Fishbeds'.

Despite suffering periodic losses, VPAF commanders were nonetheless buoyed by the 921st's apparent successes, and they decided to order its aircraft into battle in larger numbers.

The first large-scale clash took place on 23 August, following a Vietnamese radar report at 1345 hrs of a formation of 40 enemy aircraft bound for Hanoi that had been detected approaching from Xam Nua, in neighbouring Laos. Two MiG-21s and two flights of four MiG-17s were scrambled to intercept, the 'Fishbeds' launching at 1451 hrs. Nguyen Van Coc takes up the story;

'The leader, Nguyen Nhat Chieu, and I went the long way round to get into a better attacking position behind the enemy formation. He fired an AAM, bringing down a Thunderchief, while I also successfully attacked a Phantom with an R-3S AAM.

'In the meantime, the leader began another attack with his second missile but it missed. He went into cloud overhead, only to reappear moments later firing with his cannon. I also attacked the Phantom, using a missile, but I was too close, and I strayed into Nguyen Nhat Chieu's line of fire as he dived from above. My aeroplane was damaged, but all the controls were working normally so I asked to carry on the engagement. However, command ordered me to return to base – because of the damage, my MiG-21 was only able to do a maximum speed of 600 km/h.'

Although the F-105 claimed by Nguyen Nhat Chieu was listed in USAF records as having been downed by a SAM, Nguyen Van Coc's F-4D (66-0238 of the 555th TFS/8th TFW) was confirmed by American military sources as a MiG kill. Only pilot Maj C R Tyler survived the action and was captured, his WSO, Capt R N Sittner, being killed.

In comparison with the previous three months, the number of missions flown in July, August and September was down by two-thirds, although American reconnaissance aircraft remained very active, repeatedly flying the same routes over North Vietnamese airfields.

These continual overflights allowed the MiG-21 pilots of the 921st to hone their interception skills, and on 16 September two RF-101Cs were claimed by aces Pham Thanh Ngan and Nguyen Ngoc Do. Although the former's kill was credited to a SAM by the USAF, Nguyen Ngoc Do's Voodoo (56-0180 of the 20th TRS/432nd TRW) was recognised as having been downed by a MiG. Its pilot, Maj B R Bagley, was captured.

Also a six-kill ace, Nguyen Nhat Chieu claimed his second victory (an F-105D, which the USAF attributed to a SAM) on 23 August 1967. Minutes later he inadvertently damaged his wingman's jet with 20 mm cannon fire (*VPAF Museum*)

Two R-3S-armed MiG-21PFs man the alert at Noi Bai in August 1967. In the foreground, the pilot is being helped with his seat straps. His aircraft was amongst the first batch of 'Fishbed-Ds' delivered to the VPAF in April 1966 (*Vietnamese Embassy, Budapest*)

Above and right
On 17 September 1967, RF-4C 65-0894 of the 11th TRS/432nd TRW, flown by Maj John E Stavast and 1Lt Gerald S Venanzi, was shot down about 25 miles south-west of Hanoi. The VPAF credited its demise to an unnamed MiG-21 pilot, whereas the USAF stated that the jet was downed by a SAM. In the photograph above, 1Lt Venanzi's moment of capture is recreated for propaganda purposes, whilst at right, the wreckage of his RF-4 is picked over by local villagers (*VNA*)

Twenty-four hours prior to the destruction of Stavast and Venanzi's RF-4, MiG-21F-13 pilots Capt Pham Thanh Ngan and Nguyen Ngoc Do downed RF-101Cs 56-0180 and 56-0181 of the 20th TRS/432nd TRW over Son La (*VPAF Museum*)

The following day, the third RF-4C claimed by the 921st in three months was brought down.

Two MiG-21PF 'Fishbed-Ds' were scrambled against a pair of recce Phantom IIs flying at an altitude of 9000 m. Using the fighter's onboard RP-21 radar unit, the lead pilot located the first intruder some 18 kilometres ahead of him, with the second jet a further kilometre away. Selecting afterburner, he increased his speed to mach 1.4, whilst at the same time the Phantom IIs accelerated and commenced radar jamming.

Sensing that the RF-4s were on the brink of escaping, one of the MiG-21 pilots decided to try his luck with a missile shot. Flying at an altitude of 7500 m, and some 1500 m away from his target, he lined the jet up with his optical sight, fired an AAM and duly destroyed one of the RF-4Cs. Crewed by Lt Gerald S Venanzi and Maj John E Stavast, this Phantom II was claimed by the communists to be the 2300th aircraft destroyed over North Vietnam. The USAF listed the RF-4 as having been downed by a SAM.

More clashes followed in October, with the USAF losing an F-4D on the 3rd, an F-105F on the 7th and an F-105D on the 9th, all of which it attributed to MiG activity. Only the middle aircraft was claimed by the VPAF, however, this machine (63-8330 of the 13th TFS/388th TFW) being the third of ranking VPAF ace Nguyen Van Coc's nine kills. Two MiG-21s were in turn claimed by US forces – an F-4D of the 433rd TFS/8th TFW scored a kill on 24 October, followed 48 hours later by an F-4B from VF-143, embarked aboard the *Constellation*.

By November 1967, VPAF commanders had decided that in order to bring down more American aircraft, a MiG-21 from the 921st Fighter Regiment should be in the air at all times, operating from its base at Noi Bai. Nguyen Hong Nhi and Nguyen Dang Kinh were the first pilots picked for the job. At 0800 on 8 November, news came through from radar stations that F-105s and F-4s were heading for Hanoi. The two Vietnamese pilots took off from Noi Bai and set a course for the US aircraft, and as soon as the intruders spotted the MiG-21s, a section of Phantom IIs broke away from the main group and attacked.

An AAM fired by Nguyen Hong Nhi hit F-4D 66-0250 of the 555th TFW/388th TFW and turned the fighter into a fireball – its pilot, Maj W

S Gordon, ejected and was rescued, but his WSO, 1Lt R C Brenneman, was captured. Nguyen Dang Kinh also tried to attack, but his target accelerated away and disappeared into a cloud. The MiG-21 pilot did not follow, and instead cut a corner and met the US fighter with a missile when it broke from the cloud. The AAM hit its target, and the Phantom II exploded – there is no record of a second F-4 being lost to MiG activity in the USAF listings. The F-105s dropped their bombs and headed home.

More success came the way of Nguyen Van Coc on 18 November, when he and an unnamed pilot downed two Thunderchiefs that were confirmed by USAF records. This was the former pilot's fifth victory, and it took the form of F-105F 63-8295 of the 34th TFS/388th TFW. The second jet destroyed was F-105D 60-0497 of the 469th TFS/388th TFW – only the pilot of this Thunderchief survived.

The following day MiG-21s flown by future aces Vu Ngoc Dinh and Nguyen Dang Kinh claimed an EB-66 electronic warfare (EW) aircraft destroyed, although USAF records indicate that no such jet was lost on this date. These same records list F-105D 61-0124 of the 460th TFS/388th TFW as having been downed by a MiG-21 just 24 hours later, and this time the VPAF have no claim logged for the destruction of a Thunderchief on 20 November 1967.

The year would end with a flurry of engagements in December, starting on the 12th when 921st MiG-21s claimed to have destroyed an F-105 over Son Dong, in Ha Bac province – no USAF loss matches this 'kill'. Four days later F-4D 66-7631 of the 555th TFS/8th TFW was listed by the USAF as having been downed by a MiG-21, yet once again no VPAF claim was recorded.

The following day 32 F-105s and F-4C/Ds came under attack from three 'Fishbeds' whilst heading for Hanoi. Vu Ngoc Dinh claimed two F-105D kills to make him an ace, while Nguyen Hong Nhi got a third Thunderchief with an AAM. Only Vu Ngoc Dinh's first kill (F-105D 60-0422 of the 469th TFS/388th TFW) was confirmed by USAF records.

On 19 December Nguyen Van Coc claimed an F-105 over Tam Dao, while a further three unidentified types were credited to other 921st pilots. None of these 'kills' can be matched with USAF losses, however.

In 1968, the MiG-21 force was to prove even more effective. The new year got off to a good start as far as the 921st was concerned, for in early January its numbers were boosted by the arrival of 29 MiG-21 pilots who had finished their training in the Soviet Union. Their appearance was timely, as the first weeks of the year would prove to be fairly busy.

Early on 3 January, 48 American aircraft appeared over Mai Chau province, heading towards Thanh Son. A pair of MiG-21s were scrambled from Kep, flown by Nguyen Dang Kinh and Bui Duc

Nguyen Dang Kinh (left) and Nguyen Hong Nhi (right) each claimed a Phantom II destroyed on 8 November 1967, although only the latter pilot's claim was confirmed by USAF loss records. F-4D 66-0250 of the 555th TFS/8th TFW, flown by Maj W S Gordon and 1Lt R C Brenneman, was the aircraft shot down. Pilot Gordon was rescued, by WSO Brenneman was captured

Nguyen Dang Kinh and Vu Ngoc Dinh (right) were credited with the destruction of an EB-66 EW aircraft on 19 November 1967, although USAF loss records fail to confirm this claim. Both pilots are wearing a ZS-3 helmet over an SL-60 leather helmet, as well as khaki green flying suits. Notice the red patch (yellow star, no 150) and red armband (yellow star, and the wording 'Phi Cong Khong Quan Nhan Dan Viet Nam, pilot of the VPAF' stencilled on it) on Dinh's jacket for identification. The MiG-21PF behind them is armed with UB-16-57 rocket pods (VPAF Museum)

VPAF pilots of the 921st prepare for their next mission from Noi Bai. The first four are being strapped into MiG-21PFMs, while the fifth pilot is flying an elderly MiG-21F-13 (*VNA*)

Ha Van Chuc climbs aboard his MiG-21PF in late 1967. He was one of three pilots to claim an F-105 destroyed over Yen Chau on 3 January 1968, although his kill remained unconfirmed by USAF loss listings

A close up view of six-kill ace Vu Ngoc Dinh, strapped into his MiG-21PFM at Noi Bai

Nhu. The Americans were flying into the sun, and their enemy used this to their advantage when they attacked. The Vietnamese pilots lost contact with each other in the engagement, during which they each claimed an F-105. But things did not all go their way, for on returning to base Nguyen Dang Kinh overran the runway and destroyed the nose gear leg of his fighter. Further damage was caused to the cockpit of the machine when the groundcrew were forced to smash the canopy in order to extricate him. Only Nguyen Dang Kinh's claim was confirmed by USAF records, F-105D 58-1157 of the 469th TFS/388th TFW being lost.

That same day Bui Duc Nhu, who was taking turns standing the alert with Ha Van Chuc, was scrambled on another sortie, but he returned without seeing any intruders. Then, at 1500 hrs, a formation of 36 aircraft was reported to be heading for Hanoi. Ha Van Chuc took off at 1516 hrs and came across F-105s at an altitude of 5500 m. However, before he could attack he was jumped by four F-4s.

He quickly climbed to 10,000 m, and noticed that the Thunderchiefs were flying beneath him. Diving back down to 5000 m, Ha Van Chuc prepared for an attack, but the F-105s broke into him and saw him off. Undeterred, he dived on a second formation of four F-105s off to his left, but again enjoyed little success. Regaining altitude, and still looking for a target, Ha Van Chuc had just 700 litres of fuel left in his tanks.

His luck now changed, for he spotted a group of eight F-105s flying towards Tam Dao. Ha Van Chuc descended to 3500 m and attacked, getting one with an AAM – no USAF losses match his claim. On this occasion the Americans scrapped their plans to bomb Hanoi.

Two MiG-21s of the 921st, flown by Nguyen Dang Kinh and Dong Van Song, claimed the unit's second EB-66 kill on 14 January, and this time the USAF confirmed that they had lost an EW jet to MiG activity – EB-66C 55-0388 of the 41st TEWS/355th TFW. A third claim for an EB-66 was lodged by Nguyen Dang Kinh and Nguyen Duc Thuan on 3 March, but again no such aircraft is listed in USAF loss records.

Aside from the EW aircraft downed on 14 January, the air force also attributed the loss of F-105D 60-0489 of the 469th TFS/388th TFW to a MiG-21 on this day, although no VPAF pilot claimed its destruction. On 18 January two F-4Ds (66-8720 and 66-7581) from the 435th TFS/8th TFW were also downed by MiG-21s according to the USAF, but once again no official VPAF kill claims match these losses. This is also the case for F-105D 60-5384 of the 34th TFS/388th TFW, lost on 4 February, and F-4D 66-8725 of the 497th TFS/8th TFW, downed 19 days later.

However, USAF and VPAF records match for the unique F-102A loss suffered by the 509th FIS/405th FIW on 3 February, 1Lt W L Wiggins' 56-1166 being the seventh victim of Nguyen Van Coc.

After suffering an increasing number of losses at the hands of the VPAF, the USAF struck back during February, claiming MiG-21 kills on the 5th, 6th, 12th and 21st – these victories were shared by the F-4D-equipped 8th TFW and 432nd TRW.

Following this hectic start to the year, the number of aerial engagements drastically decreased in March and April. Indeed, it was not until 7 May that the VPAF claimed its next victory. This kill came about after three flights of MiG-21s, led by Dang Ngoc Ngu, Nguyen Van Minh and Nguyen Van Coc, had been sent to Tho Xuan air base. The latter pilot describes the encounter;

'My leader, Dang Ngoc Nhu, and I took off from Tho Xuan. A second pair of MiGs, flown by Nguyen Dang Kinh and Nguyen Van Lung, acted as our escorts. Because of poor co-ordination with local air defence forces, our MiGs were mistaken for

On 14 January 1968 Dong Van Song shared in the destruction of EB-66C 55-0388 (of the 41st TEWS/355th TFW) with his wingman Nguyen Dang Kinh (*VPAF Museum*)

In early May 1968 three flights of MiG-21s were sent to the 4th Military District. On the 7th of the month, two MiG-21s flown by Nguyen Van Coc (left) and Dang Ngoc Ngu (right) were scrambled from Tho Xuan, and during the course of the sortie Coc downed F-4B BuNo 151485 (from VF-92) over Do Luong (*VPAF Museum*)

Pham Thanh explains to Ho Chi Minh how he helped his colleague, Nguyen Van Coc, shoot down 1Lt W L Wiggins' F-102A Delta Dagger (56-1166 of the 509th FIS/405th FIW) on 3 February 1968

On 16 June 1968 Dinh Ton shot down F-4J BuNo 155548 of VF-102 over Do Luong, the Phantom II having launched from the *America*. The pilot of the downed jet, Cdr W E Wilber, was the CO of the unit, and he was quickly captured. His Radar Intercept Officer, Lt(jg) B F Rupinski, was killed (*VPAF Museum*)

Seeing action for the first time on 16 June 1968, Nguyen Tien Sam was flying as Dinh Ton's wingman on this day. He went on to score six kills up to 1972 (*Tran Dinh Kiem*)

American fighters, and the AAA opened up on us. This was not the only mistake – even Dang Ngoc Ngu initially mistook the escorting MiGs for Americans and dropped his fuel tanks in preparation for an attack, but he soon recognised them as North Vietnamese.

'We flew three circuits over Do Luong before being told of fighters approaching from the sea – this time they were real Americans. Dang Ngoc Ngu noticed two F-4 Phantoms five kilometres to starboard. There was a lot of cloud, and he was unable to get into a firing position. I wanted to follow him, but noticed I was running low on fuel. I was planning to land back at Tho Xuan when suddenly I spotted a Phantom ahead of me at an altitude of 2500 m. I went after him and launched two missiles from 1500 m. The Phantom crashed in flames into the sea.'

Nyugen Van Coc's seventh victim had been F-4B BuNo 151485 of VF-92, launched from the USS *Enterprise* (CVAN-65). Both crewmen were quickly recovered.

This aerial victory had been the first success for the VPAF in airspace above the 4th Military District, and from then on American aircraft regularly attacked the airfields at Vinh and Dong Hoi. Helped by the powerful air search radar fitted to their ships sailing in the Gulf of Tonkin, the Navy succeeded in controlling the airspace from Vinh Linh to Ninh Binh. When threatened by MiGs, US attack aircraft would escape by flying out to sea, occasionally luring the MiGs towards the carriers where they would be met by ship-launched SAMs. From 7 May the VPAF tried on five separate occasions to attack US cruisers and destroyers sailing just off the coast, but achieved very little for the loss of two aircraft.

One of those machines was shot down on 9 May by an F-4B from VF-96, the MiG-21 being struck by a Sparrow missile that had been fired at beyond visual range by the Navy fighter.

The next clash to take place between MiG-21s and Navy Phantom IIs occurred on 16 June. Two 'Fishbeds' operating out of Tho Xuan were flying along Highway 15 at an altitude of 250-300 m and a speed of 800 km/h when, over Nghia Dan, ground controllers told them that American jets were overflying Do Luong. Minutes later MiG-21 pilot Dinh Ton spotted four F-4J Phantom IIs, so he jettisoned his external fuel tanks, opened the throttle and commenced his attack. The MiGs and the Phantom IIs were initially closing on each other head-to-head, but the Americans suddenly chose to dive for the ground, apparently attempting to

escape. The MiGs followed them, and when the US fighters spotted the 'Fishbeds' they swung left and climbed. The VPAF pilots stuck to their prey, and as they headed out to sea, the lead jet, flown by Dinh Ton, was just 300 m behind his quarry.

He continued the pursuit, increasing his speed and firing off an AAM, while wingman Nguyen Tien Sam (encountering the enemy for the first time) provided cover. F-4J BuNo 155548 of VF-102, embarked on the USS *America* (CVA-66), was struck by the R-3S and set on fire – only its pilot succeeded in ejecting before the jet crashed. Having seen the demise of his enemy, Dinh Ton broke away from the engagement and headed for home. As the MiG-21s approached their base, Tho Xuan control tower noticed that they were being followed. However, the thought of a flak ambush convinced the US fighters to give up the chase and turn for home. For future ace Nguyen Tien Sam, it had been a lively first engagement.

The Navy exacted its revenge on 26 June when an F-8H from VF-51, embarked on the USS *Bon Homme Richard* (CVA-31), claimed a solitary MiG-21 destroyed. More success came the Navy's way on 10 July, when a pair of F-4Js from VF-33 (off the *America*) engaged three MiG-21s and succeeded in downing a single 'Fishbed'. The VPAF blamed this loss on a combination of inexperienced pilots and poor ground controlling.

MiG-21s and F-8s (from VF-111 Det 11, aboard the USS *Intrepid*) clashed again on 1 August. Nguyen Dang Kinh, Nguyen Mao and Nguyen Hong Nhi spotted their foes some 15 kilometres away, and the subsequent aerial battle took place over Do Luong, Thanh Chuong and Nam Dan. Nguyen Dang Kinh succeeded in getting behind a Crusader and fired an AAM, but it missed. Nguyen Hong Nhi then went after two other jets, launching a missile at a distance of 1000 m whilst in a banking turn at an angle of 60°. The Navy pilot was himself turning at an angle of 45° when the AAM was fired, and it flew harmlessly by. However, Nguyen Hong Nhi reported hitting the Crusader with a second round fired seconds later – no F-8s were lost on this day according to the Navy.

A second Crusader then started a turning fight with Nguyen Hong Nhi, closing to within 2500 m. The MiG pilot pushed open his throttle and banked sharply to the right, before initiating a climb. However, the

Seen at Noi Bai in May 1968, the MiG-21PF closest to the camera was used by ranking VPAF ace Nguyen Van Coc to down F-4B BuNo 151485 of VF-92 over Do Luong on 7 May 1968. This victory represented Coc's seventh, of nine, kills. Following the release of this photograph to the world's press in mid 1968, several western publications claimed that the 13 red stars on the fighter's nose denoted the success of a single pilot, namely the fictitious 'Colonel Tomb'. In fact, these markings represented the victories of a number of 921st pilots up to that stage in the war. Note the uniquely camouflaged MiG-21PFM taxiing out from the dispersal area (*VNA*)

Between them credited with the destruction of 23 American aircraft, Capt Pham Thanh Ngan (centre) demonstrates manoeuvres to Nguyen Duc Soat (left) and Nguyen Van Coc (right) for this undoubtedly posed propaganda photograph. The three aces are walking along the ramp at Noi Bai in late 1968. Behind them are parked MiG-21PFM 'Fishbed-Fs', armed with R-3S missiles. Note how VPAF pilots had abandoned the uncomfortable one-piece g-suits in favour of g-webbing by this stage of the war. The full face helmet was also discarded at the same time (*Vietnamese Embassy, Budapest*)

high g-loading was too much for his 'Fishbed', and he was forced to abandon this manoeuvre and perform a 30° banking turn to the left when he realised that the American was firing cannon shells at him.

The F-8 pilot followed him, and he was just 300 m behind the MiG when Nguyen Hong Nhi attempted to turn inside him to avoid being hit. After three tight turns, he finally found himself behind the F-8, but an intermittent electrical malfunction prevented Nguyen Hong Nhi from firing his remaining missiles.

At that moment two F-8s from VF-51 arrived on the scene and opened fire. Nguyen Hong Nhi again tried to climb out of trouble, but this time his fighter was hit by two Sidewinder missiles and he was forced to eject. He returned to his unit three days later, where he announced that before take-off he had noticed that the throttle of his fighter was not working properly, but he decided not to report it before launching.

On 19 September there was another encounter involving two MiG-21s, and again an electrical fault with the flight leader's jet prevented him from firing his missiles. His wingman claimed an F-8C destroyed, however. No losses were recorded by the Navy, which in turn credited a pilot from VF-111 Det 11 with a single MiG-21 kill. On 26 October a solitary F-4 was also claimed by the 921st, although no losses were again reported by US forces.

The US government declared a bombing halt on 1 October, followed by a ban on all overflights of North Vietnam, except by reconnaissance aircraft, on 1 November. Attacks on communist targets in Laos and South Vietnam would continue, however.

As a result of this halt, fighter engagements were drastically scaled down. Indeed, aside from downing the odd Firebee drone, the only action of note involving the MiG-21 in 1969 occurred on 9 February when two jets from the 921st Fighter Regiment departed Noi Bai, bound for Vinh. They were reportedly attacked by American fighters en route, and forced to head for Tho Xuan instead. One of the aircraft ran out of fuel prior to landing and the pilot ejected.

With US bombing raids continuing into Laos, the VPAF moved a handful of MiG-17s and -21s south to bases at Vinh and Anh Son, within

the 4th Military District, in March 1969. Pilots chosen to serve in this district received additional flying training, and by 6 April the unit at Anh Son had attained combat readiness. This training had been tailored for operations in the south, with ten ex-MiG-17 pilots being drawn from the 921st to transition onto the MiG-21MF (Type 96) 'Fishbed-J'. Five of these men concentrated on mastering bad weather flying, while the remaining pilots received instruction on night flying.

One of the principal aircraft involved in the bombing campaign in South Vietnam and Laos was the mighty B-52, and the MiG-21 pilots now based at Vinh had orders to attack any intruding Boeing bombers. On 22 April a pair of MiG-21s were transferred to Anh Son, which was the VPAF airfield closest to the Laotian border. However, these fighters were poorly camouflaged once they had landed, and soon after being spotted by US recce aircraft they were destroyed in an American bombing raid.

Successes were few and far between over the next few months. On 28 January 1970, two MiG-21s were patrolling Route 12 after taking off from Vinh when they intercepted an F-4. Pham Dinh Tuan quickly 'downed' the jet (no US losses support this claim), while his wingman, Vu Ngoc Dinh, destroyed HH-53B 66-14430 of the 40th ARRS, which had been orbiting over Laos waiting to head into North Vietnam to rescue the crew of a downed F-105G. This was the first reported incursion of a VPAF MiG-21 into Laotian airspace, and also the only loss of a US helicopter to an AAM during the war.

Pham Dinh Tuan failed to make it safely back to his base, for his fighter crashed into a mountain in bad weather during the pilot's approach to landing, killing him instantly.

On 28 March, the Americans launched several air strikes on the airfield at Muong Xen in response to increased MiG activity in the area, and due to bad weather, the unit at Tho Xuan could not scramble any aircraft to defend the base – four MiG-21s were hastily launched from Kien An instead. Two of the North Vietnamese pilots had no

The 921st 'Sao Do' began to receive new MiG-21MF (Type 96F) 'Fishbed-Js' in early 1969, and within weeks of the jets' arrival ten VPAF pilots had transitioned onto the type with the help of Soviet instructors

Mai Van Cuong was credited with eight kills between 1966 and 1968. In this view, the restricted forward vision out of the cockpit of the 'Fishbed' is readily apparent. Both the radar scope and the optical sight above it are clearly visible. Cuong is sat in the cockpit of a MiG-21PFM 'Fishbed-F' (*VPAF Museum*)

Nguyen Van Coc (front) leads the charge down the flightline at Noi Bai in 1969. Judging by the smiles on the faces of the pilots, this is yet another event staged for the camera. Coc destroyed two Firebee drones with his MiG-21PFM during the course of December 1969 (*VNA*)

This photograph was possibly taken on the same day as the shot above. Here, pilots from the 921st conduct an impromptu pre-flight brief on the flightline in late 1969. They are all wearing winter-issue flying suits and ZS-3 helmets (*VNA*)

combat experience whatsoever, and one of them was shot down over Ninh Binh by an AAM fired from an F-4J from VF-142, embarked on the *Constellation*.

In the dry season of 1971, as the Vietnamese Army's 559th Corps transported supplies for their troops in the south along Route 9, the VPAF was instructed by Hanoi to distract the attention of B-52s and AC-130 gunships away from the ground forces. This would prove to be a difficult task, for the MiG-21 pilots were unfamiliar with Route 9, and links with ground control were inadequate.

Air force commanders picked veteran MiG-21 pilot Dinh Ton to take part in the action, for they believed his vast experience would allow him to cope with the poor weather conditions that plagued the area. On one of his early flights he departed from Noi Bai at 1700 hrs and then recovered at Dong Hoi to refuel. Taking off again at 1900 hrs, he headed for Route 9, but the Americans had by then become aware of his flight and pulled all of their AC-130s out of the area for good.

VPAF missions against the B-52s met with less success in the first half of 1971, however, so several air force officers were sent to Mu Gia Pass to observe B-52 attack patterns both during the day and at night. In September of that year, radar units were sent to Ba Don, in Quang Binh province, and to Vinh Linh to track B-52 activities.

On 4 October, commanders of the 921st sent Dinh Ton to Dong Hoi, from where he would go 'hunting' B-52s. The pilot took off after sunset, but the USAF crews were effectively jamming all communications in the area and he had to fly without ground radio contact. Dinh Ton soon found two B-52s in front of him, but judged the situation unsuitable for combat and diverted to Tho Xuan.

On 20 November, two more MiG-21s were sent to Vinh, and another jet to Anh Son. At 2000 hrs that same day, B-52s were reported 60 kilometres to the north of Xam Nua. Pilot Vu Dinh Rang was about to become the first fighter pilot within the VPAF to intercept a B-52.

At 2046 hrs he scrambled from Anh Son airfield, and once aloft he was informed by ground control that his three targets were 100 kilometres away. He dropped his fuel tanks and climbed to 10,000 m, and at a distance of 15 kilometres, Vu Dinh Rang switched on his radar and applied full throttle. At eight kilometres he fired an AAM at one of the B-52s, and as he broke away from his attack, he spotted another bomber in front of him. Vu Dinh Rang launched his second missile, and at 2115 hrs he landed at Anh Son. There, he was told that the first B-52 had been damaged and had had to make an emergency landing in Thailand.

The attempt to shoot down B-52s, as well as an increased movement of North Vietnamese troops towards the south, prompted President Richard Nixon to warn Hanoi that bombing strikes would re-commence if such activities continued. As part of this threat, fighter-bombers started penetrating North Vietnamese airspace once again, and on 18 December the VPAF struck back when Le Thanh Do and Vo Si Giap downed F-4Ds 66-0241 and 65-0799 of the 432nd TRW.

The air war in Vietnam was about to reach a dramatic climax.

As the VPAF's leading ace, Nguyen Van Coc was liberally decorated with awards throughout the war. Each of the nine badges pinned to his right breast denote an aerial victory (*VPAF Museum*)

On 18 December 1971, two F-4Ds (66-0241 of the 555th TFS/8th TFW and 65-0799 of the 13th TFS/432nd TRW) fell victim to the 921st's Le Thanh Dao (right) and Vo Si Giap (left). Here, the victorious pilots recount the action to technicians

Below left and right MiG-21US/UM 'Mongols' were used to practise for night missions mounted against B-52s in late 1971. Pilots had to be ready to take off within six minutes during daylight hours, and seven minutes at night, should bombers be detected. The VPAF was desperately short of night-qualified pilots, with only 13 out of a total of 194 pilots being cleared for nocturnal flight

THE CLIMAX

By the beginning of 1972 all pilots in the 921st Fighter Regiment had converted onto the MiG-21MF (Type 96) 'Fishbed-J', and an increasing number had been trained for combat in adverse weather and at night. The unit's command centre had also been moved to Bach Mai, while a stand-by unit was based at Chuong My, in Ha Tay province. The policy now was for every regiment to have a back-up command group that would be able to step in and take control of an air battle at any time.

And 1972 would see the VPAF's MiG force fighting plenty of 'air battles', as USAF and Navy fighters attempted to gain aerial supremacy over North Vietnam as part of Operation *Linebacker*.

The escalation in hostilities in the north following almost three years of relative quiet commenced in the final months of 1971, and gathered pace in the first quarter of 1972. With the North Vietnamese Army (NVA) attempting to hide preparations for its new spring offensive against South Vietnam, overflights by US reconnaissance aircraft flying *Blue Tree* missions began to be opposed more frequently. The Americans responded by conducting more frequent, and progressively heavier, protective strikes.

The first MiG-21 kill claimed by US forces since March 1970 fell to future Navy aces Lt Randy Cunningham and Lt(jg) 'Willie' Driscoll, flying with VF-96 (equipped with F-4Js) off the *Constellation*, on 19 January 1972. USAF F-4Ds (all from the 432nd TRW) then downed the next six 'Fishbeds' to be claimed, on 21 February, 1 and 30 March, and 16 April. The aerial battle on the latter date had seen the VPAF launch no fewer than 30 fighters (ten MiG-21s, six MiG-19s and fourteen MiG-17s), which attempted to protect Vietnamese supply convoys near the border with South Vietnam. Three MiG-21s were destroyed, and the loss of so many jets on a single day persuaded VPAF commanders that their forces should restrict their fighting to north of the 20th Parallel, where they could rely on adequate SAM protection and ground control.

Nevertheless, the 921st continued operating with MiG-21MFs over the 4th Military District, but it also remained available for missions over the north at any time.

Following the escalation in the air war, the VPAF had formed a second MiG-21-equipped unit on 3 February 1972, namely the 927th 'Lam Son' Fighter Regiment. Equipped with MiG-21PFM (Type 94) 'Fishbed-Fs', the unit was tasked with operating north of the 20th Parallel in support of the 921st, which was now led by eight-kill ace Nguyen Hong Nhi.

Revitalised by new equipment and better tactics, the US air forces had downed seven MiG-21s and a solitary MiG-17 without suffering a single casualty in the first four months of 1972. This all changed on 27 April.

Hoang Quoc Dung and Cao Son Khao of the 921st had departed Noi Bai and set a course for Vu Ban. Soon after take off, they detected a pair of F-4Bs some six kilometres in front of them. The MiG pilots quickly closed to within three kilometres of the Phantom IIs, and at this point Hoang

On 3 February 1972, the 927th 'Lam Son' Fighter Regiment was established under the command of ace Nguyen Hong Nhi, who was credited with eight kills between 1966 and 1972 (*Tran Dinh Kiem*)

27

Quoc Dung fired off a missile at one of the jets. The R3S struck F-4B BuNo 153025 of VF-51, embarked on the USS *Coral Sea* (CVA-43), and the fighter burst into flames and crashed. The jet's Radar Intercept Officer (RIO), Lt Cdr James B Souder, remembers;

'The day I was shot down I was on my third carrier cruise, flying my 335th mission in Navy F-4Bs in Vietnam. I was 31 years old, a lieutenant commander Radar Intercept Officer, and had over 1000 hours in the F-4. My pilot was a young lieutenant named Al Molinare.

A pilot from the newly-established 927th Fighter Regiment demonstrates to fellow aviators the standard flight formation used during engagements with American aircraft. The 927th was established with MiG-21PFM 'Fishbed-Fs'

'That particular day we were designated to fly as wingman for a senior pilot. We were scheduled, and planned, to bomb a target near Hanoi, but the weather was bad – there was a solid overcast all around Hanoi, which extended more than 60 miles to the south, so we were diverted to a bridge target a little north of Vinh. We were armed with Sparrow and Sidewinder AAMs, and each aircraft carried four cluster bomb units. En route to the target we destroyed a truck heading north on Highway 1. We arrived over the target and set up a TARCAP station a little west of it at 8000 ft, some 90 miles south of Hanoi. We moved up into position and flew alongside our leader.

'After a few minutes, our air-intercept controller made the call, "Vector 360 at 85". Apparently, a single MiG-21 had just taken off from Phuc Yen airfield, or had just popped up on the controller's radar 85 miles away from us. "Roger that", our wingman said, and steadied up, heading 360°.

'There was a solid cloud layer at 3000 ft between us and the MiG, and I figured he would be below it, and we'd never see him. I took a look at the chart I always kept with me, and looked out the front windscreen. I said, "Ok Al, do you see that lake up there about half way to the horizon that looks like a finger?" Al saw it through the break in the undercast.

'"Well, it's called finger lake, and we're going to meet the MiG right over it, or a little north of it, and this looks like a trap". I was thoroughly convinced of it myself, as my mind immediately went back to a scenario I'd

Above and below
Three-tour veteran Lt Cdr James Souder poses in the back seat of his F-4B aboard the USS *Coral Sea* in early 1972. Assigned to VF-51, and teamed up with first-tour pilot Lt Al Molinare, he was shot down by Hoang Quoc Dung of the 921st 'Sao Do' on 27 April 1972 (*via J B Souder*)

developed five months earlier about a situation where the MiGs might try to trick us into a fight on their terms. This was the right weather condition, this was the right terrain, and this was the right aeroplane – an F-4B which didn't have a pulse-Doppler radar with look-down capability . . . and I figured the MiG pilot knew we were an F-4B, or he wouldn't be foolish enough to come right at us like he was.

'I looked at my chart again and noted that our track would take us

The MiG-21PFM closest to the camera has been painted light grey overall, and it lacks a tactical 'Bort' number as worn on the natural metal MiG-21MF 'Fishbed-J' parked behind it. Both jets are about to undertake a night training sortie as part of the VNAF's attempt to have a cadre of pilots capable of intercepting the B-52s that bombed the north during the hours of darkness (*VNA*)

When Hungarian Premier Jenö Fock visited the 921st and 927th Fighter Regiments in 1972, Deputy Minister for National Defence, Lt Gen Károly Csémi (centre), presented the Hungarian Army flag to Col Tran Hanh, CO of the 'Sao Do' regiment (*Vietnamese Embassy, Budapest*)

just east of Bai Thuong airfield, a new MiG base which had been built since I was last in-theatre in 1967.

"'360 at 75'" . . . "'360 at 70, speed point 6'", announced our controller. The MiG was steadily getting closer, heading directly toward us, loping along at 360 knots.

"360 at 65". This was exactly the type of MiG intercept scenario that I had discussed with a friend just a few months earlier, but it was going to be further complicated by our low fuel state. I knew intuitively that one of the planes in this flight would not return that day. I began formulating a plan of action to follow in case our plane was fatally hit. We were still too far out in range to start trying to find the MiG with my radar, so I had time to figure out where we should go if we were hit and couldn't make it to the water, where we would most likely be picked-up.

"'360 at 60'". I remembered telling our leader one day that the VPAF would take advantage of the F-4B's radar by flying under clouds and hiding in the ground clutter, as they had often done back in 1966 and 1967.

On 27 April 1972, the 921st Fighter Regiment's Hoang Quoc Dung took off from Noi Bai and engaged a pair of F-4B Phantom IIs from VF-51. He fired a single R-3S missile at the Navy fighters, and BuNo 153025 burst into flames and crashed. Pilot Lt Al Molinare and RIO Lt Cdr James Souder both successfully ejected and were subsequently captured. This was Dung's only known kill of the conflict

'"360 at 45" . . . "360 at 40. Speed 360". I thought to myself that the MiG pilot must be either a 2nd lieutenant or a brave old-timer, because he just sat there and calmly kept coming at us, obviously not afraid at all to take on a pair of Phantoms single-handedly. But he had every advantage in the world going for him – he was in his own friendly sky, under his own friendly clouds, over his own friendly territory, talking to his own friendly controller, expecting to meet us right near one of his own friendly MiG bases, where lots of friendly help may be waiting to launch, and we were broadcasting our presence to him with our own unfriendly big, black, five-mile-long smoke trails.

'"360 at 30". It was getting to be time to start looking with the radar. A MiG-21 is a little aeroplane and it has a tiny radar signature, and it would have been useless to be searching for him before now. We still sat there at 8000 ft. I started searching with the radar.

'"360 at 25". I told my pilot to go down to 7000 ft.

'We were still in combat spread, with us on the right, about a mile-and-a-half abeam of our leader. I kept looking for the MiG on the radar, but I didn't see a thing. My leader stayed at 8000 ft, at 420 knots, smoking like a freight-train. We should have left him right then, but it's a wingman's job to stay with his leader, no matter how bad the situation gets.

'"360 at 20". I searched all over, but couldn't find the MiG.

'"360 at 15". During training, they had told us about smoke control, and we'd figured that out for ourselves as far back as 1962 – the aeroplane smoked like a coal stove. So now we knew to go into minimum afterburner in order to get rid of the F-4's smoke trail. It was obvious to any pilot that our big, black smoke trail was a deadly tip-off to an adversary. If we didn't do it, the MiG pilot could spot that five-mile-long black plume that trailed behind us and sneak out to the side and around us, and up from below us, to get behind us and blow our butts off – and by now surely the MiG pilot must already have us in sight.

'The right time had already passed for us to go into min-burner, and anyway, *now we didn't have the fuel to do it!* Our two planes were right now passing just off the eastern end of Bai Thuong airfield.

'"360 at 10". I tried to see under the clouds and over the terrain, but there was too much ground clutter. I knew I couldn't find a three-square-metre target looking down on to him over North Vietnam.

'"360 at 4". I knew that radar plots could easily merge as far out as five miles, so at the "360 at 4" call I abandoned the radar and took a long look inside the section's rear area at my leader's six o'clock, in case the MiG had gotten ahead of the controller's radar's slow sweep. I looked level, below and above, trying to cover all the area between the two aircraft, just like I was supposed to do.

'I could have said, and I *should* have said, "Your six is clear", to my wingman, which may have tipped him off to check my six in case he wasn't checking it, but for some reason I didn't say anything. Then I swung around and looked behind us to the right, outside the section, level, low and high. As I was looking back, our controller announced, "Whoops, he might have slipped behind you. Check 220 at 4".

'I swung my head back through the cockpit and darted my eyes at the heading indicator to confirm 220 was at my seven o'clock position, and BAM! Suddenly there was a loud noise, no shuddering or vibration, just a

loud noise, and the plane immediately started to slow down. Apparently, an Atoll missile had just slammed into the aeroplane, disabling both engines. I was thrust forward in my ejection-seat straps, and it felt just like when you're going at supersonic speed and you come out of afterburner. I stepped on the UHF switch and told my leader that we'd been hit.

'"This is 2. We've taken a hit and we're going down".

'I then looked left in the 220 direction to see if the MiG was threatening our leader but I didn't see it. Then I looked back out to the right and saw the narrow, straight, brilliant white plume of exhaust gases left by a second AAM that had just streaked by beneath our right wing. My mind realised the reality of the situation, but it had a hard time accepting it.

'Intellectually, I knew it had to be an Atoll, but I hadn't actually seen a MiG. My intellect simply wouldn't accept it. It was too hard for me to believe after over 335 missions, and all the missions I'd gotten away with totally unscathed, that on a simple, almost benign flight like this, a MiG had actually gotten me.

'I said, "Turn left for the mountains, Al. What's going on with the engines?" He replied, "The left one's at 30 per cent and the throttle is frozen. It won't move. The right one is at idle and the throttle is sloppy, like it's disconnected – it isn't doing anything".

'Our Phantoms had rear-view mirrors on them, which were mounted outside on the front arcing metal rim of the RIO's canopy. I never found them to be of much use in finding aeroplanes behind us, but it sure worked for another purpose now. I looked in it and saw that the whole rear-end of the plane was burning. The fire seemed to be shooting out at least 20 ft to the sides as best I could tell, and we were doing just 250 knots – that was some fire!

'"We're burning like hell Al, but fly this thing until it comes apart", I said. My studies of F-4 shoot-down reports instantly came back to me, and I knew that the jet had a reputation for not exploding even when it was burning badly . . . if it hadn't exploded upon first being hit. This was the time to gamble. We really needed to fly as far as we could before ejecting. Al said "Okay".

'Al finally started a turn, but it was a right turn. I was trying to get Al to turn left in an attempt to get him to head for the relative safety of the mountains. The mountains were much safer for a helicopter extraction than the open land beneath us and to the east. The Jolly Greens could get up there to the mountains easily, but they wouldn't dare come out this far into the open flatlands, nor right by a MiG base!

'"Al, what are you doing?" I said. "Uh, I'm trying to get to the water".

'The plane was now in a 30° banked turn to the right, passing about 030 heading. '"What do the hydraulic gauges say?" "They're all zero". If he pushed the stick over to reverse our turn, it would probably pump

Hoang Quoc Dung's MiG-21PFM taxies towards the runway at Noi Bai at the start of the 27 April 1972 mission that would see him down Molinare and Souder's F-4B over Vu Ban. Behind the 'Fishbed' are several overall grey and overall green MiG-21PFMs, none of which display 'Bort' numbers (*Vietnamese Embassy, Budapest*)

out all the residual hydraulic fluid we had left in the flight-control systems and we'd lose control of the plane and have to eject before we reached the mountains.

'We continued the right turn, gliding slowly downward at 250 knots. I switched the radar to stand-by and stowed it out of my way in preparation for the ejection. As we passed through 180 degrees Al said, "There he is. There's the MiG".

'"Where?" I asked, as I pulled out my radar from its stowed position and switched it back on. "The son of a bitch got us but we can still get him. Where is he?" I was in wide sweep and level antenna and looking at the scope, but I didn't see a thing. "Ah, he's off the scope. He's out there at three o'clock. He's heading north".

'I looked out to my right, hoping to spot the MiG with my naked eye, but no MiG. I slammed the radar back to its stowed position and this time I turned it off. I had to laugh at myself a little for trying to get in a shot at the guy who'd already shot us down, but after all, that's what we'd been trained to do, wasn't it?

'Our jet was disabled, and no doubt we were going down, but we still had electricity from the generators and the radar was working, and if the MiG had been on my scope, we'd have used up the last bit of hydraulic fluid to pull the nose around, and we'd have shot that bastard down too. Hell, we were over his country – he could hitch a ride back to Phuc Yen.

'Just as we steadied up to the west, Al said, "Okay, I'm going to lose it, we're going to do a roll to the right. Get it on the upside". I looked out at the left wing and saw the flight spoiler standing in its full-up position. "Okay, I've got you selected". We had already agreed that I would eject both of us when/if the time came, and I had the command/select handle in the "both" position, which meant that when I pulled my eject handle, I'd take Al with me – and this was the time.

'The plane started a slow roll to the right just as the altimeter needle passed 3000 ft. I straightened my spine, grabbed the lower ejection handle with my right hand and gripped my right (*text continues on page 49*)

Top and above
Before and after. In the photograph at the top of this page, VF-51's F-4B BuNo 153025 is seen during a training mission (note the blue practice bombs on the underwing ejector racks) off the coast of southern California just weeks prior to embarking on the *Coral Sea* in November 1971 and heading for the Tonkin Gulf. In the shot immediately above, Vietnamese militiamen attempt to salvage the remarkably intact tail section of 'Screaming Eagle 102' from a field near Vu Ban. This was the only Phantom II lost in combat by VF-51 during its eight-month-long 1971-72 deployment. The unit also claimed four MiG-17s destroyed whilst operating from *Yankee Station* (*via J B Souder and the Vietnamese Embassy, Budapest*)

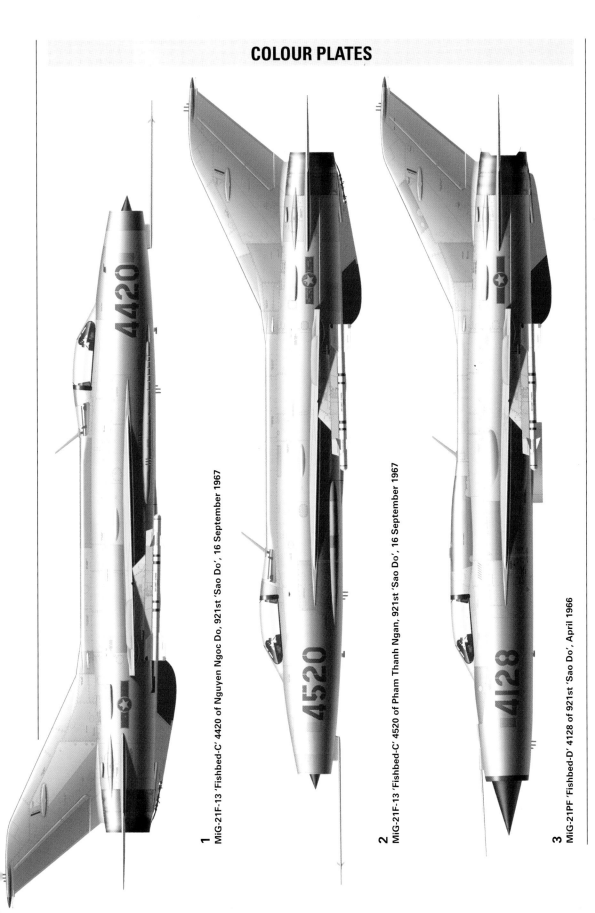

1
MiG-21F-13 'Fishbed-C' 4420 of Nguyen Ngoc Do, 921st 'Sao Do', 16 September 1967

2
MiG-21F-13 'Fishbed-C' 4520 of Pham Thanh Ngan, 921st 'Sao Do', 16 September 1967

3
MiG-21PF 'Fishbed-D' 4128 of 921st 'Sao Do', April 1966

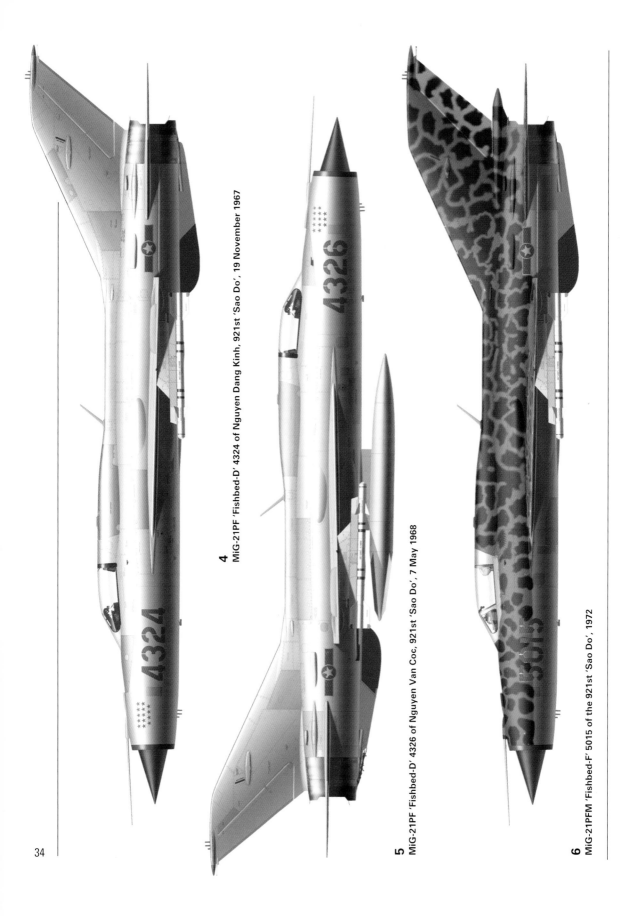

4
MiG-21PF 'Fishbed-D' 4324 of Nguyen Dang Kinh, 921st 'Sao Do', 19 November 1967

5
MiG-21PF 'Fishbed-D' 4326 of Nguyen Van Coc, 921st 'Sao Do', 7 May 1968

6
MiG-21PFM 'Fishbed-F' 5015 of the 921st 'Sao Do', 1972

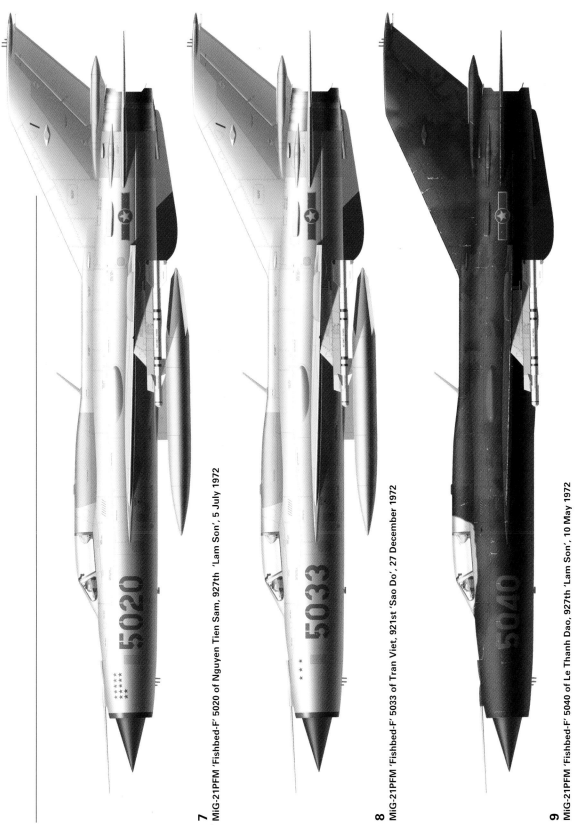

7
MiG-21PFM 'Fishbed-F' 5020 of Nguyen Tien Sam, 927th 'Lam Son', 5 July 1972

8
MiG-21PFM 'Fishbed-F' 5033 of Tran Viet, 921st 'Sao Do', 27 December 1972

9
MiG-21PFM 'Fishbed-F' 5040 of Le Thanh Dao, 927th 'Lam Son', 10 May 1972

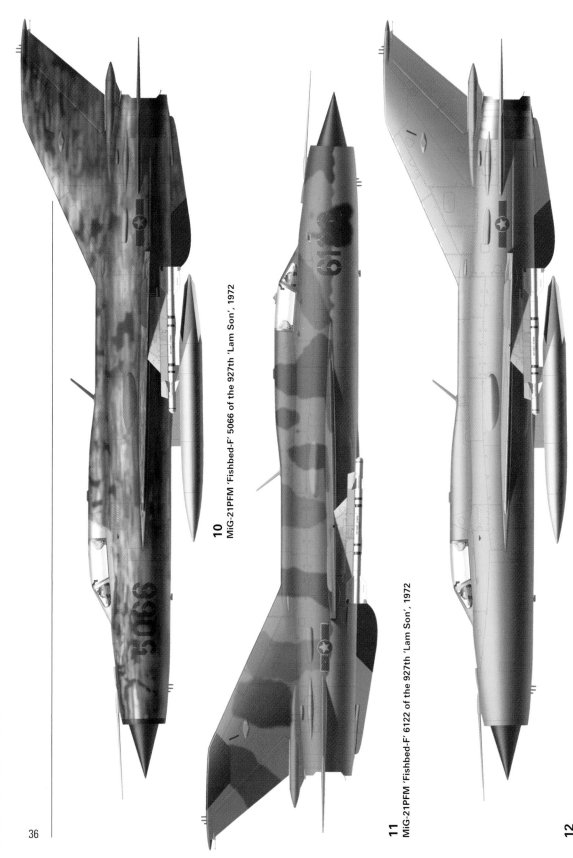

10
MiG-21PFM 'Fishbed-F' 5066 of the 927th 'Lam Son', 1972

11
MiG-21PFM 'Fishbed-F' 6122 of the 927th 'Lam Son', 1972

12
MiG-21PFM 'Fishbed-F' (no Bort number) of the 921st 'Sao Do', 1972

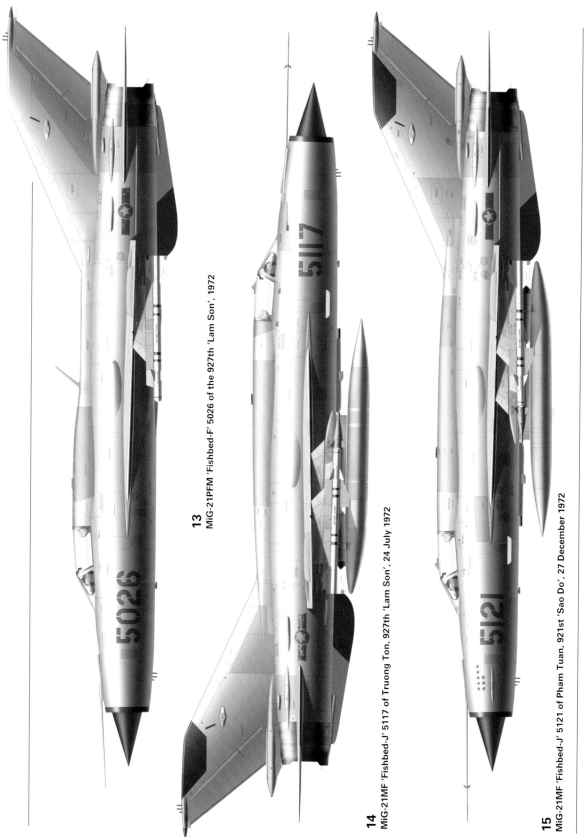

13
MiG-21PFM 'Fishbed-F' 5026 of the 927th 'Lam Son', 1972

14
MiG-21MF 'Fishbed-J' 5117 of Truong Ton, 927th 'Lam Son', 24 July 1972

15
MiG-21MF 'Fishbed-J' 5121 of Pham Tuan, 921st 'Sao Do', 27 December 1972

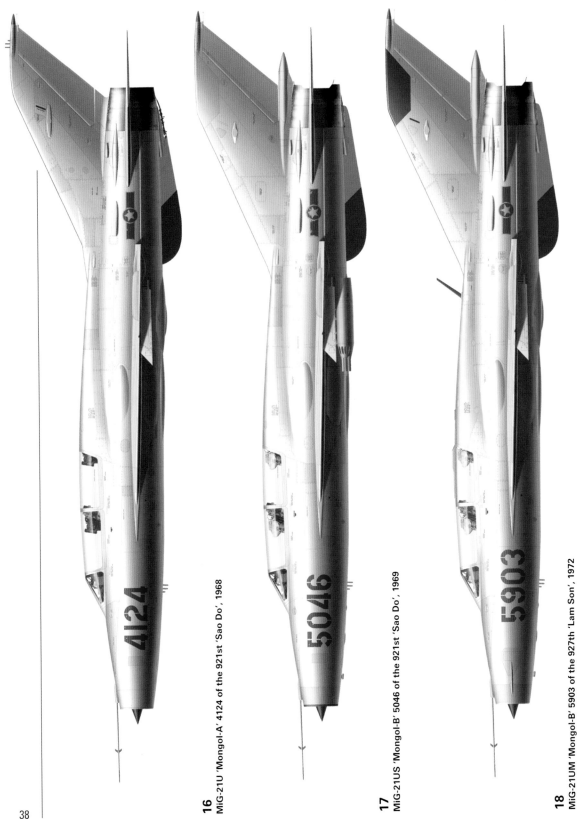

16
MiG-21U 'Mongol-A' 4124 of the 921st 'Sao Do', 1968

17
MiG-21US 'Mongol-B' 5046 of the 921st 'Sao Do', 1969

18
MiG-21UM 'Mongol-B' 5903 of the 927th 'Lam Son', 1972

1

2

3

4

5

6

7

8

9

10

11

12

13

14

15

43

16

17

18

NORTH VIETNAMESE STAMPS

Stamp 2

Stamp 1

Stamp 3

Stamp 4 (two stamps)

Stamp 5

Stamp 6

Stamp 7 (two stanps)

Stamp 8 (two stamps)

Stamp 9 (two stamps)

Stamp 10

Stamp 11

Stamp 12

Stamp 13

Stamp 14

Stamp 15

Stamp 16

Stamp 17

Stamp 18

Stamp 19

Stamp 20

Stamp 21

46

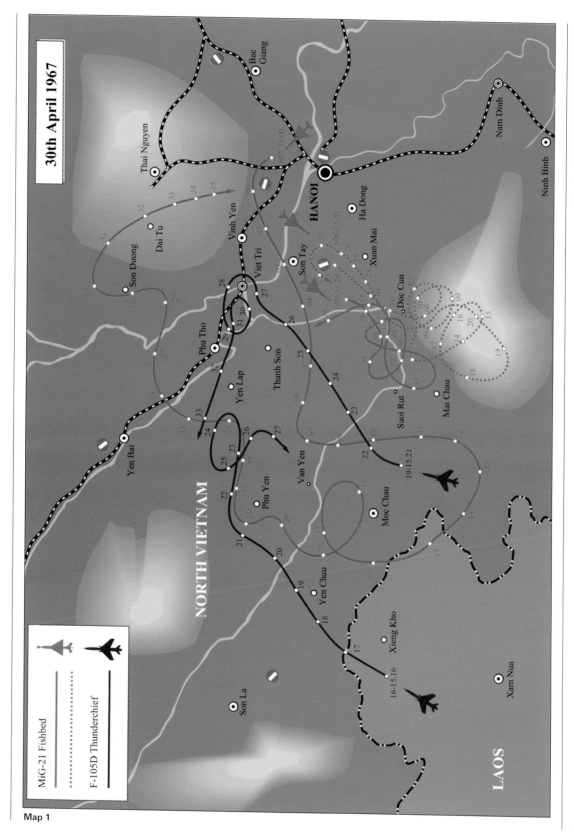

Map 1

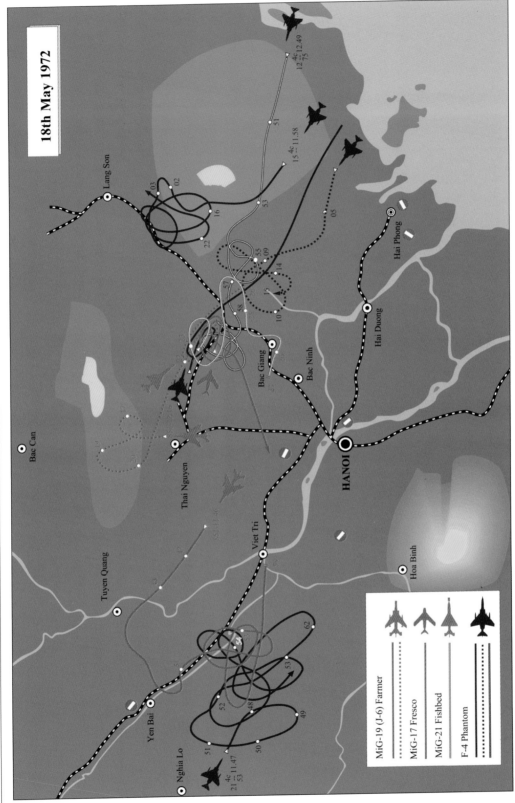

18th May 1972

MiG-19 (J-6) Farmer

MiG-17 Fresco

MiG-21 Fishbed

F-4 Phantom

Lang Son

Bac Can

Thai Nguyen

Tuyen Quang

Yen Bai

Nghia Lo

Viet Tri

Bac Giang

Bac Ninh

Hai Duong

Hai Phong

HANOI

Hoa Binh

wrist with my left hand, tucked my elbows in as close to my sides as I could and just followed through on the roll.

'As the plane rolled through the inverted position and continued on to the desired 45° to go to wings-level position, I jerked the handle – "BAMM" went the canopy, "thwoosh" went the rocket-seat, then I think I did a back flip, I'm not sure, then "thut, thut, thawump", and I was hanging in my parachute about 1500 ft above the ground. I had always wondered what it'd be like to make a parachute jump, and after all the explosions of the actual ejection and 'chute deployment, I was immediately struck with how quiet and calm it was.

'I looked up and checked the canopy and lines, which all looked okay to me. It was surprisingly pleasant – a soft ride, quiet, no rush of the wind, and I thought, "If I get out of this mess, I'm going to do this again someday". I looked down and saw the aeroplane directly below me in a giant fireball. I looked off to my left and I saw Al hanging there in his 'chute. I rolled my helmet forward off my head and dropped it, then took my hand-held radio out of my survival vest and called my flight-leader.

'"This is 2 Bravo. I'm out of the aeroplane and I'm okay".

'"Roger that. Well, about all I can tell you is to try to make it to the mountains over there".

'"Roger, I understand. I gotta go".

'I put my radio in my survival vest as bullets continued to whiz by, making those little sonic booms as they went. Why the MiG pilot chose me to shoot down rather than my leader, I didn't know, but I would wonder for a long time during the next 11 months I was to spend in prison in Hanoi.'

In the wake of the Spring Offensive launched by the NVA on 30 March, US aircraft had been attempting to disrupt the southerly progress of the invasion as part of Operation *Freedom Train*. Initially, strikes were only allowed against targets south of the 19th Parallel, but on 10 May Operation *Linebacker I* was launched, which approved sustained attacks on targets north of the 20th Parallel. The whole of North Vietnam could now be bombed.

At the time of the launch of *Linebacker I*, the MiG-21 force was concentrated at Kep, Yen Bai and Hoa Lac, while the aircraft at Anh Son were in the process of moving to Mieu Mon. The technical personal at Vinh and Anh Son were evenly divided between the 921st and 927th Regiments, while the supporting 45th Radar Company received reinforcements from the 921st and the 43rd Radar Company welcomed personnel from the 927th. Finally, high command ordered personnel of the newly-established 26th Radar Company into the control towers at both bases.

Four days prior to the instigation of *Linebacker I*, two MiG-21s had been downed by a pair of F-4Js from VF-114, embarked on the USS *Kitty Hawk* (CVA-63). On 8 May, pilots from the 927th became embroiled in a dogfight over Yen Bai. Pham Phu Thai and Vo Si Giap of the 921st were also in the air at the time, having received orders to distract the Phantom IIs as they headed for Tuyen Quang.

The MiGs were in the process of attacking the F-4Ds (from the 432nd TRW) in the hope of holding up at least some of them when Giap received a missile hit – the round was almost certainly fired by F-4D 65-0784, crewed by the 555th TFS's Maj Robert Lodge and Capt Robert Locher. This pairing had already downed a MiG-21 on 21 February 1972, and

would claim a third MiG-21 on 10 May. However, they would be shot down just minutes later by a MiG-19, and although WSO Locher ejected and was recovered, pilot Lodge crashed to his death.

Returning to 8 May, Vo Si Giap was ordered to eject, but he found himself overflying a heavily-populated area so he elected to make an emergency landing at Thuong Trung after locating a suitable clearing. Giap had failed to spot the school on one side of the open ground, however, and children streamed out of the classrooms when they heard his aircraft. Giap's first thought was to avoid them, and as he made a turn away from the field his aircraft exploded.

The following day, both the 921st and 927th were given the job of defending the railway bridge between Hanoi and Lang Son, as well as bridges along Route 5 at Lai Vu and Phu Luong.

The NVAF had quickly realised in early 1972 that its opponents had closely analysed the performance of its MiG fighters during the three years of vitual inactivity, and devised new tactics in order to negate the strong points of the Soviet-built designs. For example, when dealing with the MiG-21, F-4 crews were told to lure the 'Fishbed' pilot into a horizontal dogfight, and to avoid vertical manoeuvring .

A clutch of 921st 'Sao Do' pilots walk from their MiG-21PFM 'Fishbed-Fs' at Noi Bai after completing a regiment-wide training mission. An unusually camouflaged MiG can just be seen parked in the line-up behind the aviators, the jet featuring mottled dark green uppersurfaces over natural metal undersides (*VPAF Museum*)

Looking more strained than the individuals seen above, these 927th pilots have just finished a patrol over Hanoi. They are both wearing ZS-3 'bonedomes' over SZ-60 leather helmets, plus the standard-issue leather flying jacket. The second pilot is also carrying a KM-32 oxygen mask in his hands (*Vietnamese Embassy, Budapest*)

On 8 May 1972, during a dogfight with an overwhelming number of 432nd TRW F-4Ds over Thuong Trung, the MiG-21 of the 921st's Vo Si Giap was struck by a missile and critically damaged. Realising that he would not make it back to base, Giap attempted to land in a nearby clearing, but as he was his final approach he spotted a school below him and he turned away. His aircraft exploded seconds later and he was killed

A MiG-21UM 'Mongol-B' two-seat trainer of the 927th heads a row of 921st MiG-21MF 'Fishbed-Js' at Noi Bai in the spring of 1972 (*Tran Dinh Kiem*)

Flying with an increased combat spread of 900 m, a pair of Phantom IIs could keep a far better look-out for each other, and sound a warning in the event of an imminent MiG-21 attack. By this stage the Americans had also discovered that the 'Fishbed' could out turn the F-4 at medium and high altitudes, but that the Phantom II had the advantage 'down low'. F-4 crews were duly instructed to dive to a lower altitude as soon as they encountered a MiG-21. Both the USAF and the Navy proved just how much their tactics had improved on 10 May.

That morning aircraft attacked Hai Phong, Bac Ninh, Pha Lai, Son Dong and Luc Ngan, and ignored Tu Ky and Ninh Giang due to the presence of MiG-21 fighter cover. Scrambled in response to these strikes, 921st 'Fishbed' pilots Dang Ngoc Ngu (ultimately a seven-kill ace) and Nguyen Van Ngai had just departed Kep when they were surprised by a flight of F-4s from the 432nd TRW. Nguyen Van Ngai was immediately shot down, but Dang Ngoc Ngu somehow managed to avoid the missile meant for him and climbed to 1000 m. He quickly radioed a warning to Le Thanh Dao and Vu Duc Hop, who were about to take off.

He then saw two Phantom IIs in front of him and jettisoned his fuel tank, which damaged his control surfaces when it came away. Dang Ngoc Ngu applied full power, increasing his speed from 900 to 1100 km/h just as the two F-4s split up – one went into a climb and the other made a horizontal turn. The MiG-21 went after the latter jet.

At a distance of 1200 m, the seeker head of the AAM locked on to the Phantom II and Dang Ngoc Ngu fired the weapon, shooting down F-4E 67-0386 of the 58th TFS/432nd TRW – both crewmen were killed. He swiftly turned his attention to the climbing Phantom II, but his second missile was jammed on the launch rail. Dang Ngoc Ngu's opponent made the most of his good fortune by applying power and slipping away. At 0912 hrs the veteran MiG-21 pilot landed his damaged fighter at Noi Bai.

Elsewhere, strike aircraft were attacking targets north of Hanoi, while a group of fighters kept a close watch on the MiG bases at Noi Bai, Hoa Lac and Kep. Two 921st 'Fishbeds' that succeeded in scrambling from Noi Bai headed for Tuyen Quang in a bid to distract the Americans' attention.

On approaching their destination the VPAF pilots spotted six F-4s flying in pairs over Tuyen Quang. The wingman was told to attack, and he managed to destroy one Phantom II prior to being downed himself by a 'friendly' SAM unit – the MiG crashed, killing the pilot. No loss within US records matches this claim.

The flight leader also received 16 20 mm cannon hits from the American fighters, but he was determined to save his aircraft. He managed a slow descent, flying around Tam Dao mountain while gradually decreasing his altitude and eventually landing at Noi Bai.

The 10th would also bring the 927th 'Lam Son' Fighter Regiment its first taste of victory after the unit's MiG-21PFMs were scrambled. Ground control informed Le Thanh Dao and Vu Duc Hop that there were American aircraft flying passing some 35 kilometres to the west of Hai Duong, at an altitude of 3500 m. Le Thanh Dao duly looked around and noticed a black dot in front of him. He ordered Vu Duc Hop to jettison his fuel tank, and in turn opened his throttle. Soon he was clearly able to see the Phantom IIs' smoke trails.

The F-4Js split up, one of them making a left turn and passing beneath Dao, while the other one turned back and went into a climb, only to be followed by the MiGs. Vu Duc Hop launched an AAM from a distance of 1500 m, and he was about to fire a second when he saw that he had hit the target. He yelled 'Success', before turning left and decelerating.

Looking ahead, he spotted another F-4 bracketed by heavy flak. Keen to press home another attack, Vu Duc Hop was prevented from doing so by ground controllers who feared another 'friendly' fire incident. He was ordered to land at Kep for his own safety.

Meanwhile, Le Thanh Dao had been chasing after another F-4. Closing to within 1500 m, he launched a single AAM which struck the Phantom II and turned it into a fireball. He too then turned homeward. The 'victims' of both these attacks had been F-4Js from VF-92 and VF-96, off the *Constellation* (the latter jet flown by newly-crowned aces Randy Cunningham and 'Willie' Driscoll). And according to the Phantom II crews involved, the VF-92 jet was downed by AAA and the VF-96 machine by a SAM. In return, a second F-4J from VF-92 had claimed a solitary MiG-21 destroyed during this encounter.

The 921st's Dang Ngoc Ngu was one of the longest serving MiG-21 pilots in the VPAF, seeing action from 1966 though to 1973. During this time he claimed seven US fighters destroyed, the first in May 1967 and the last in May 1972 (*VPAF Museum*)

Two MiG-21PFMs are scrambled from Noi Bai during the intense fighting of mid-May 1972. Both jets are armed with a pair of K-13 Atoll AAMs, and lack a centreline drop tank. The absence of the latter indicates that the 'Fishbed' pilots have been sent aloft on an airfield defence mission (*Vietnamese Embassy, Budapest*)

10 May had witnessed some of the fiercest aerial battles of the war, with USAF crews claiming three MiG-21s destroyed and the Navy seven MiG-17s and a single MiG-21. The 'Fishbed' pilots had been credited with four Phantom II kills, and the Americans had admitted the loss of an F-4D to a MiG-19 and an F-4E to a MiG-21.

In an effort to counter the new US tactics, the VPAF introduced attack flights patrolling at altitudes of between 300 and 800 m, operating in conjunction with deception flights at ceilings of 8000 to 10,000 m. The two-aircraft sections would patrol some ten to fifteen kilometres apart.

While aircraft in the 'dummy' flight would fly at just 900 km/h, the attack group would patrol at 1200 km/h. Both flights stayed in airspace under radar control, receiving their orders from the command centre.

There was no respite for either side following the massive battles of 10 May, and less than 24 hours later the 927th Fighter Regiment again found itself in combat. At 1430 hrs the USAF launched 26 aircraft against Bac Mai airfield. From this group, eight jets would attempt to neutralise the SAM batteries surrounding the base, while a further two flights of four aircraft monitored activity at nearby Noi Bai, Ba Vi and Hoa Lac airfields.

Two pairs of MiGs from the 927th were scrambled from Noi Bai, with the attack pair of Ngo Van Phu and wingman Ngo Duy Thu flying at a height of just 500 m on a southerly heading in an effort to intercept US aircraft heading for Hanoi. Meanwhile, the pair carrying out the deception flight flew towards Tuyen Quang and Van Yen to engage the enemy over Hoa Lac and Yen Bai.

Two minutes into the flight, Ngo Duy Thu detected a single US aircraft five kilometres away. Moments later, ground control ordered the flight to jettison its fuel tanks. The pair increased speed, and Ngo Duy Thu spotted a further four enemy aircraft off to his left at an altitude of 7000 m and a distance of 15 kilometres. Ngo Van Phu was also aware of the aircraft, and ordered his wingman to attack. Banking tightly to the right, Ngo Duy Thu closed on an F-105G some 1200 m away and immediately launched a missile, scoring a kill.

Maj William H Talley of the 17th WWS/388th TFW was the pilot of the Thunderchief (62-4424) struck by the AAM;

'Flying F-105G Wild Weasels, our flight was supporting a strike in the Hanoi area. I was flying at approximately 15,000 ft when I was shot down by a MiG-21 shortly after noon, local time.

'I turned my aircraft to the south-west and got approximately 25 miles from Hanoi before bailing out. I landed on the side of a mountain and climbed to the top to await rescue. However, the rescue attempt was not made until mid-morning of the following day. I was captured just as the rescuers flew into the area where I was hiding. They tried to rescue my backseater, but were

The entire pilot and groundcrew strength of the 927th Fighter Regiment march by during a parade to mark the formation of the unit at Noi Bai in February 1972. Note the uniform equipment of all 24 pilots (*Vietnamese Embassy, Budapest*)

On 10 May 1972 Le Thanh Dao was credited with scoring the 927th's first victory when he 'shot down' an F-4J off the *Constellation* over Hai Duong. However, the official US Navy records for this day state that one Phantom II from VF-92 suffered a direct hit from AAA, while a jet from VF-96 (flown by aces Randy Cunningham and 'Willie' Driscoll) was downed by a SAM. Having also served with the 921st, Le Thanh Dao was credited with six kills between December 1971 and September 1972 (*Vietnamese Embassy, Budapest*)

Ngo Duy Thu discusses the dogfight of 11 May 1972 with Lt Col Joseph W Kittinger, who had been shot down by Ngo Van Phu while flying F-4D (66-0230 of the 555th TFS/8th TFW). Thu had himself destroyed F-105G 62-4424 of the 17th WWS/388th TFW on this mission. Kittinger had earlier been credited with a MiG-21 kill on 1 March 1972

driven away by MiGs in the area. My backseater was also captured, and we both were both held as prisoners-of-war until 28 March 1973.'

While Maj Talley was being brought down, a hard right turn saved Ngo Duy Thu's MiG from an American missile. He duly went after another F-105, but he was too close to his target (just 600 m away). Indeed, facing a 60° launch angle, he was unable to fire an AAM. Following orders from ground control, Thu broke off the fight, lost height and followed the Da River to Noi Bai.

His flight leader, Ngo Van Phu, had also been involved in a tussle with the USAF, intercepting four F-4Ds of the 555th TFS/432nd TRW that had been escorting the main group of F-105s. He launched two AAMs in quick succession from a distance of 1500 m, and F-4D 66-0230 was duly hit. The crew ejected and were captured – the downed pilot, Lt Col Joseph W Kittinger, had himself claimed a MiG-21 on 1 March 1972.

Attempting to break away from the remaining trio of Phantom IIs, Ngo Van Phu felt his MiG-21 shake violently as it was struck by an AAM. Activating his SK-1 ejection system, the VPAF pilot was shot clear of the stricken aircraft and he drifted safely down to earth. The destruction of Phu's MiG-21 was never officially credited to a single crew, as in the confusion of battle all three F-4s had fired missiles at the jet.

By analysing the battles of 8-11 May, and interrogating captured US aircrewmen, the VPAF high command and the chiefs of staff concluded that the Americans were trying to destroy, or at least paralyse, the VPAF.

Improved US tactics now saw fighters laying in wait in the vicinity of VPAF airfields, and they would attack as soon as the MiGs took off. At first this threw the North Vietnamese pilots and controllers into confusion, despite them having prior knowledge of these strikes. This resulted in the communist pilots attempting to engage enemy fighters using outdated tactics, while lacking any co-ordinated control from the ground.

Furthermore, a good number of the MiG-21 pilots were seeing combat for the first time. And although there were now two regiments equipped with 'Fishbeds', there was little communication between units.

Alarmed by mounting losses, the party leadership in Hanoi met with VPAF commanders and formulated a strategy to hit back at the enemy, while at the same time modernising the air force. Discussions focused on better communication between the VPAF and ground units of the Air Defence Forces, and also between radar and communication units.

In mid-1972 the VPAF's main forces were operating north of the 20th Parallel. In order to preserve air force strength, and ensure its long-term fighting capability, defences were increased around jet storage facilities. In addition, the number of MiGs on alert was cut from between 32-34 to 12-16.

Whilst these high level meetings were taking place in Hanoi, further

clashes continued to occur. On 18 May four MiG-17s from the 923rd Fighter Regiment, along with a flight of MiG-19s from the 925th and a pair of MiG-21s from the 927th, were involved in an engagement with intruders over Kep. The leading MiG from the 927th, flown by ex-921st ace Nguyen Hong Nhi, was chasing a Phantom II when he suddenly changed his heading and downed a second F-4 over Kep. This was Nhi's eighth, and last, kill, although it was not confirmed by US loss listings.

Two days later a pair of MiG-21s from the 921st sortied from Noi Bai and attacked a formation of 12 F-4Ds from the 555th TFS/432nd TRW over Suoi Rut and Phu Ly. Wingman Do Van Lanh managed to dodge an AAM before launching both his missiles and claiming F-4D 65-0600. Both crewmen ejected safely. The pilot of the Phantom II, 1Lt John D Markle, had earlier downed a MiG-21 during the epic clashes of 10 May.

On 23 May both MiG-21 regiments were in action, with an unnamed pilot from the 921st claiming the destruction of an F-4D that the USAF listed as having been hit by a SAM. In return, the crew of an F-4E from the 35th TFS/366th TFW claimed a MiG-21 shot down. VPAF ace Nguyen Duc Soat, now flying with the 927th, was also credited with the destruction of A-7B BuNo 154405 from VA-93 (off the *Midway*) on this day, although the Navy state that this jet was probably downed by a SAM.

Twenty-four hours later the 921st saw yet more combat, scrambling two pairs of MiG-21s. The first two jets flew north-west towards Thai Nguyen, and although both launched AAMs, they failed to score due to the pilots' lack of experience. The second pair flew south and met up with American aircraft over Vu Ban, and again the leader used up both his heat-seeking missiles without success. On the way back to base, pilot Do Van Lanh noticed he had almost no fuel left. Adamant that he was not going to lose his jet, he decided to take a risk, and from a distance of 45 kilometres and an altitude of 5500 m, he set his throttle to idle. His faith in himself and his aircraft paid off, and he glided in safely at Noi Bai.

Although the VPAF failed to lodge any claims on 24 May, the Navy stated that the loss of F-8J BuNo 150311 from VF-24 (off the *Hancock*) was caused either by a SAM or an AAM fired from a MiG.

The carnage of May 1972 finally came to an end on the 31st when single 'Fishbeds' were downed by an F-4D and an F-4E from the 432nd TRW. One of the victorious pilots was the 555th TFS's Capt Paul Ritchie, who had just destroyed the second of five MiG-21s that he would be credited with between 10 May and 28 August.

In the wake of these dreadful losses, the VPAF called a conference in late May for the commanders of the MiG regiments, and other senior officers, at which lessons learned from the recent dogfights would be discussed. Within two weeks a report was ready, analysing enemy tactics and manoeuvres, as well as the current state of the VPAF, and its combat readiness. The report also made recommendations for dealing with Vietnamese shortcomings in the air. It was immediately distributed among the MiG pilots. In light of this crisis meeting, perhaps it was no coincidence that in the second half of 1972 the MiG-21s of the 921st and 927th inflicted far greater losses on the USAF and Navy, although both regiments still suffered their fair share of setbacks.

June started positively for the 921st when, on the 1st, two MiG-21s intercepted twelve F-4Es between Suoi Rut and Viet Tri. The leader of the

The 921st's Do Van Lanh came tantalising close to becoming the VPAF's 14th ace, for he was credited with downing four Phantom IIs between 20 May and 9 September 1972. He was honoured with the nickname 'The Ironbird' by his fellow squadron pilots, this sobriquet having been previously bestowed upon ranking Vietnamese ace Nguyen Van Coc (*VPAF Museum*)

Do Van Lanh climbs aboard a 921st MiG-21MF 'Fishbed-J' in mid-1972. 'The Ironbird's' third kill took the form of F-4E Phantom II 69-0282 of the 334th TFS/8th TFW, which he downed with a single R-3S AAM on 21 June 1972. Its crew, pilot Capt G A Rose and WSO 1Lt P A Callaghan, were captured

section, Pham Phu Thai, fired an AAM and then broke away in a stunning 9.5g turn in an airframe designed to withstand a maximum of 7gs! He still managed to safely land the jet. Thai claimed an F-4 destroyed, although the USAF stated that the fighter had been hit by a SAM.

On 10 June two 921st MiG-21s claimed a kill over an undisclosed type, which could not be confirmed by the official US loss listings. Seventy-two hours later, four more 921st machines engaged F-4Es of the 308th TFS/432nd TRW over Vinh Phu, and on this occasion flight leader Pham Phu Thai's claim of a single Phantom II destroyed was confirmed by the USAF – 67-0365 was lost to an AAM, its crew ejecting and being captured. Second pair wingman Do Van Lanh also stated that he downed an F-4, but the Americans list only one loss for the 13th.

Lanh was more successful – at least in terms of having his claimed verified by the USAF – on the 21st, when two MiG-21s from the 921st scattered a fighter group which failed to reach its intended target. Flying as a wingman once again, he downed F-4E 69-0282 of the 334th TFS/8th TFW. In separate engagements fought elsewhere on this day, the crew of an F-4E from the 469th TFS/388th TFW claimed a MiG-21 destroyed, as did F-4J-equipped VF-31, embarked on the USS *Saratoga* (CVA-60).

The MiG-21 force would enjoy better results on 24 June. A pair of jets from the 927th was scrambled against American fighters that had approached Thanh Son from the north-west. Ordered aloft too late to intercept the enemy jets, they were set upon by the USAF F-4s within minutes of taking off. Unable to contact his wingman via the radio, the flight leader took on the Phantom IIs alone but failed to score a kill.

Detecting more aircraft inbound, the 927th launched additional flights of refurbished MiG-21MF (Type 96) 'Fishbed-Js' as the American intruders attacked the industrial area at Thai Nguyen, as well as several other targets on Route 1 between Lang Son and Hanoi.

The USAF formations followed a route over Phu Tho, Yen Bai, Hoa Binh, Cho Ben and Son Dong, and at 1512 hrs Nguyen Duc Nhu and Ha Vinh Thanh took off to intercept the intruders over Thanh Son. Ground control ordered the pilots to distract the Americans.

When the USAF formation had reached an area to the north-west of Phu Tho, a single fighter section broke away and started to chase the MiGs. By this time Ngo Duy Thu and Nguyen Duc Soat had also been scrambled, and when they caught up with the US fighters, the latter pilot launched an AAM at one of the jets, which crashed (F-4E 68-0315 of the 421st TFS/366th TFW was the second of six kills credited to Soat).

He then attempted to get the flight leader, but found that he was too close, and despite dropping away from the F-4, he still failed to achieve a missile lock. The remaining Phantom IIs banked sharply right and lost height in an attempt to pull the MiG-21s down to their favoured dogfighting altitude. However, Nguyen Duc Soat was wise to this tactic, and broke off the engagement and returned to Noi Bai.

In the meantime, Ngo Duy Thu had also managed to claim an F-4 from another fighter group (not confirmed by USAF loss listings). Faced with more targets, he increased his speed and altitude, before diving at the American formation once again. Targeting the lead aircraft, Thu's high speed and angle of attack was too great for his AAM, and the missile failed to make contact. He too then fled back to Noi Bai.

At 1542 hrs Nguyen Van Nghia and Nguyen Van Toan launched in their MiG-21s, and once again the VPAF jets were immediately set upon by USAF F-4s. Despite this, Toan still managed to fire off an AAM at one of his assailants, but the missile failed to guide. Nguyen Van Nghia then successfully locked up a second Phantom II, firing off a single R-3S from a distance of 1200 m, before pulling up sharply. F-4D 66-7636 of the 25th TFS/8th TFW crashed in flames.

The USAF hit Hanoi again on 27 June, with 44 aircraft being sent against a variety of targets. Amongst the latter were the airfields at Noi Bai and Gia Lam, and 12 F-4s intercepted VPAF MiGs over Nghia Lo and Vinh Phu as they in turn attempted to stop F-105s that were knocking out radar units crucial to the Vietnamese fighters' ground control system.

Nguyen Duc Nhu and Ha Vinh Thanh were the first to take off from from Noi Bai on this day, and Nhu was credited with the destruction of an F-4E that the USAF claimed was destroyed by a SAM.

More Americans fighters arrived on the scene a few minutes later, heading for Hoa Binh, Thanh Son, Moc Chau, Van Yen and Son La in flights of twos and fours at an altitude of 5000-6000 m. The detection of these aircraft resulted in the scrambling of Nguyen Duc Soat and Ngo Duy Thu, who took off mid-morning from Noi Bai and headed immediately for Hoa Binh and Van Yen. Pham Phu Thai and Bui Thanh Liem also launched at this time, and they were directed to Yen Bai and Nghia Lo.

En route to Hoa Binh, Soat and Thu spotted four American aircraft in front of them, as well as four more sections approaching North Vietnamese airspace from the west, some 40 kilometres from the Laotian border. Ignoring those jets already ahead of them, the MiG pilots turned back, climbed to 5000 m and waited for the aircraft nearing the border. Heading towards a pair of F-4s just a few kilometres away, cruising at 3000 m, the VPAF pilots requested permission to attack.

At a distance of 1500 m, Nguyen Duc Soat fired off a missile and hit F-4E 67-0248 of the 308th TFS/432nd TRW. The first round caused the Phantom II to emit a thick smoke trail, but the fighter failed to catch fire. However, a second heat-seeking missile launched just seconds after the first finished the job, and the USAF jet burst into flames and crashed. Nguyen Duc Soat immediately turned for home.

His wingman, who had also been chasing an aircraft of his own, duly turned his attention to a second section of F-4s off to his left. Thu fired two AAMs and claimed one jet destroyed (not listed by the USAF). By now running low on fuel, he effected an emergency landing at Hoa Lac.

Pham Phu Thai and Bui Thanh Liem had also run into a four-ship formation of USAF Phantom IIs over Nghia Lo, but these aircraft dived into cloud after spotting the VPAF fighters. A few minutes later Thai spotted an F-4 off to his left, another one making a banking left turn and two pairs breaking off to the right. He told Liem to keep an eye on the two jets to the left, since he reckoned they would try to sneak back behind them.

When they were sure that nobody was following them, the Vietnamese pilots repositioned themselves in a staggered-level formation and closed on the two F-4s to the right of them. From a distance of 1300 m, Pham Phu Thai launched a single AAM, while Bui Thanh Liem chose to fire his R3S from 200 m further away. Both missiles tracked perfectly, hitting F-4Es 69-7271 and 69-7296 of the 366th TFW.

Nguyen Van Nghia of the 927th claimed five kills during the bitter *Linebacker I* **clashes near Hanoi in mid-1972 (***Tran Dinh Kiem***)**

These 'Fishbeds' all belong to the 927th, and they are seen at Noi Bai during the summer of 1972. The pilots are strapping into a mix of single-seat MiG-21PFMs and MFs and two-seat UM 'Mongol-Bs'. At least three of these fighters have been crudely oversprayed with green paint in an effort to camouflage them (*VNA*)

Capt Thomas J Hanton was the WSO in 69-7271 (call sign 'Valent 04'), which was targeted by Pham Phu Thai;

'For the morning mission on 27 June, our wing was tasked to provide three flights of four to escort both the chaff-laying flight and bomb droppers, with one flight of four (all of the four-ship flights were made up of F-4Es) conducting the Barrier Combat Air Patrol (BARCAP).

'The flight joined up with the string of four flights of F-4s over the Plain de Jars area of north-eastern Laos. The "gorilla" (attack formation) would ingress along Route Package VI from the west. One of our sister units (the 421st TFS) established a four-ship BARCAP along the Laos-North Vietnam border, while a second four-ship from this unit took the lead escort position on the left side, 45° back from the chaff-laying flight.

'The second of our squadrons (the 4th TFS) supplied the other two escort flights, and they formed up in a staggered "out-rigger" formation on either side of the bomb droppers. The mission commander had placed two escort flights on the left side of the formation, where the air threat was believed to be greatest, and the other one on the right side about line abreast with the lead flight of F-4 "bombers".

'Our three F-4 flights rolled in on their target and egressed back west. "Valent" flight then turned to chase a two-ship of MiGs, after first jettisoning our empty centreline fuel tanks. The MiGs must have decided the odds weren't favourable, or the element of surprise was lost, for they went for the deck. We couldn't close with the MiGs to get a visual – all we had was a 25-nautical-mile radar contact. We ended up making a wide sweep between Hanoi and Hai Phong, then fell in-trail with the egressing 12 F-4s, and continued on to our tankers for the post-strike refuelling.

'While on the post-strike tanker, the flight was directed to contact "King", the call sign of the C-130 airborne command post co-ordinating the Search and Rescue (SAR) for the aircrew of the two downed aircraft from the morning mission. We were given an area back in North Vietnam, north-east of Hanoi, to provide fighter cover for a Fast Forward Air Controller (FAC).

'The solitary Fast FAC was an F-4E (hence called fast, to differentiate it from other FACs who used slow aircraft, such as the OV-10, in Laos and South Vietnam) flown by a highly experienced crew that was down low conducting both a visual search for 'chutes and a radio search for a survivor's voice or beacon.

'The BARCAP flight had been sent in immediately, and we would end up cycling in and out with them in concert with two cycling Fast FACs. We were given the Fast FAC's radio frequency to contact so we could co-ordinate our CAP and cycle times. He was already in the area, so we took up our CAP in our assigned area. The idea was to patrol around the enemy skies, keeping a watch for any MiGs that would prey on both the Fast FAC and the vulnerable rescue force.

The USAF suffered one of its worst maulings at the hands of these MiG-21 pilots during attacks on Hanoi on 27 June 1972, with at least three F-4Es (and possibly as many as five – the Americans list two jets downed by SAMs, which the VPAF claim to have destroyed) being downed by VPAF fighters. These pilots are Nguyen Duc Soat and Ngo Duy Thu (left) from the 927th, and Pham Phu Thai and Bui Thanh Liem (right) from the 921st. The latter pair each claimed a Phantom II from the 366th TFW, while Soat destroyed a jet from the 308th TFS/432nd TRW

'Even if we saw the Fast FAC, we would avoid orbiting directly over him so his position, and that of any survivors, would not be revealed. As we ingressed the area, "Disco" called out Blue bandits (the American code for MiG-21s), using Hanoi as the bull's eye.

'The flight lead immediately had us drop our remaining external wing tanks and turn toward Hanoi in the direction of the bull's eye call. We ended up in another tail chase. This high-speed chase and dumping of wing tanks containing fuel meant it was time to hit the tanker again.

'Following another air refuelling – our third of the day – we headed back into North Vietnam. With only internal fuel, and far north of the closest recovery base in Thailand-Udorn, we would reach bingo fuel after no more than a single circuit through our CAP area. In combat, we based our bingo on the minimum fuel needed to reach a divert base and be able to make two approaches. We had clear weather today, so had a low bingo fuel. In any other weather condition we would have been heading home.

'We arrived back in our CAP area and made a blind call to our Fast FAC that "'Valent' is on station with four". As we approached the centre of our area, I queried about our fuel. The pilot (Lynn Aikman) answered by transmitting over the radio, "'Valent Four', bingo!" The flight lead did not provide any confirmation, which was not unusual since radio calls were kept to a minimum, but continued steering east towards Hanoi.

'One of the challenges the flight lead has, particularly with a flight of four, is manoeuvring the formation. In combat, you do not want to keep your aeroplane flying in a straight line for any longer than half your altitude above the ground in seconds. Today, that equated to ten seconds.

'Because the threat was from the air, our flight lead modified this to 15 seconds, which meant we were moving the aircraft frequently, and not just cruising around. Not only did this provide a less predictable target to any North Vietnamese threat, but it allowed us to roll up on a wing and check below the flight. This constant manoeuvring, added "g" to make the manoeuvre and the addition of power to the engines meant we used up fuel fast. An additional problem for "blue four" was that always being

Nguyen Duc Soat relates details of his Phantom II kill on 27 June to his squadronmates from the 927th Fighter Regiment. This was Soat's third kill, and he would go on to double this number by mid-October 1972 (*Tran Dinh Kiem*)

on the extremes of the turns meant more throttle jockeying to maintain position. This caused us to have the lowest fuel state in the flight.

'We were rapidly approaching emergency fuel – the absolute minimum fuel needed to exit the area and climb to a maximum endurance altitude from which to start a long glide to the closest runway! Both bingo and emergency fuel were based upon not being able to air-refuel. Since we had had three previously successful refuellings, it wasn't as critical as it could have been, but there were no guarantees. I was more vigilant than ever, for a month earlier two of us had flamed out on our landing roll-outs after pushing the fuel reserves too far. And "Valent" lead was continuing east!

'If we got tapped by a MiG we'd have little fuel to either fight or do any *defensive* manoeuvring, which would really require a lot of fuel. Again Lynn transmitted, '"Valent four", Bingo minus 1". We were 1000 lbs below bingo, and just 1000 lbs from emergency fuel. Finally, we turned back to egress. With our low fuel state, Lynn was forced to use altitude to dive and cut off the flight because the jets were turning away from us, which immediately threw us out of formation. Simultaneous with the turn came another "Disco" "Blue bandits" call.

'I had the centre co-ordinates of our CAP area as the number one way-point of the inertial navigation system, which I was displaying on our flight heading system, and the centre of Hanoi (the bull's eye) as the secondary way-point. Disco's radio call cued me to switch over to the bull's eye way-point to determine how far behind us that put the MiGs. I calculated 15 nautical miles – not an immediate threat. But I still directed the pilot to give me a deep six check.

'As he rolled up on the right wing, turning into the three members of our flight that were a couple of hundred feet above us as we tried to gain airspeed by diving, I would look low and down behind us. The dive would give us the airspeed and some cut-off angle to pull back up into formation while conserving fuel – a sound manoeuvre in this situation. We finished neither the manoeuvre nor got the look.

'Instead, we got *hammered*. That's what it felt like. As if a giant had slapped the back end of the jet with a big hammer. My head was rotated about three-quarters of the way around, and Lynn had about ten degrees of bank when the pilot hosed off an Atoll infra-red heat-seeking missile.

'There was no doubt in my mind what had happened. The aeroplane shook and spun out of control as the left engine burned and the hydraulic lines controlling the flight control systems were severed. I assumed the ejection position and pushed my helmet hard against the head cushion of the ejection seat to prevent it from being rattled around the cockpit, and to allow my eyes to focus on the altimeter.

'If the aircraft wasn't stabilised by 15,000 ft on the altimeter, I would pull the ejection handle as covered in our crew briefing. It was coming fast. I raised my right hand from the ejection handle, located on the ejection seat between my legs (I continued holding it with my left hand) in order to feel the control stick – it was as limp as a piece of wet spaghetti. Before I could reach back to the ejection handle to pull with both hands, I went "up the rail". The pilot had initiated our ejection. For some unknown reason we had lost cockpit intercom when the missile hit, so I got no warning. Fortunately, I was mostly in the correct ejection position.

'For the next nine months I was a PoW in the "Hanoi Hilton" and "Zoo" prisons. I was released to US military custody on 27 March 1973.'

Despite suffering considerable losses during the spring and early summer of 1972, the VPAF commenced further training programmes in July. This move clearly showed that the air force was capable of both fighting the enemy and training new pilots. Most of the latter would be trained to fly the MiG-21MF, receiving conversion training on the MiG-17.

A significant player in Operation *Linebacker* was the B-52, examples of which were attacking targets across the north at night. Neither the MiG-17 or -19 could touch the high-flying Boeing bomber, so it was left to the MiG-21 to deal with this deadly threat. The Vietnamese chiefs of staff approved an attack plan against the B-52 in mid-1972, and 12 pilots (eight of them trained for night missions) were chosen to execute it.

Training flights in the MiG-21MF were performed in all types of weather, day and night, and from short landing strips. By the end of the year, all 12 pilots were ready to tackle B-52s at altitudes up to 10,000 m.

Whilst this training was going on, senior VPAF commanders were also having to deal with the improved, and constantly changing, tactics of the USAF and Navy fighter-bomber force that was battering targets in the north. Ground control radar sites were particularly hard hit, with the Americans jamming signals and attacking both permanent and mobile units with anti-radiation missiles. However, some of the VPAF's problems were self-inflicted, for certain unit commanders despised the enemy so much that they became over-confident in battle, causing heavy losses.

Communist party chiefs attempted to deal with this by instigating a new policy whereby any problems encountered in-flight were thoroughly analysed after each mission. In particular, any sign of a pilot becoming cocky and showing a lack of respect for the enemy's ability was seriously frowned on. Hanoi feared that if this sort of attitude continued, the VPAF would suffer some really serious losses.

The policy of going back into battle right after a defeat was also criticised. Pilots, it was recommended, should learn the lessons of their previous engagements, and from them draw up fresh and more effective tactics before they got back into the cockpit. As the fighting continued, senior officers hoped the strategy would work. Sometimes it did, but sometimes things would go wrong.

An example of things going right, on 5 July, resulted in the VPAF claiming its first kills since 27 June. Nguyen Tien Sam and Ha Vinh Thanh of the 927th Fighter Regiment engaged two F-4Es from the 34th TFS/388th TFW over Ha Bac. Firing at a distance of 2000 m, Sam's first AAM exploded shortly after it had been launched, but he pressed home his attack and shot off a second round from just 1000 m behind his foe. F-4E 67-0296 exploded. Moments later Ha Vinh Thanh also fired off two R-3Ss, destroying F-4E 67-0339.

The final fiery moments of F-4E 69-7296 of the 366th TFW, shot down by the 921st's Bui Thanh Liem over Nghia Lo on 27 June. The crew of the Phantom II, pilot Maj R C Miller and WSO 1Lt Richard H McDow, both successfully ejected. Miller was subsequently rescued by a USAF SAR team, but his WSO was captured before he could be extracted (*VNA*)

CHAPTER THREE

The 921st's seven-kill ace Dang Ngoc Ngu claimed his final victory on 8 July, when he destroyed F-4E 69-7563 of the 4th TFS/366th TFW. Its crew ejected and were recovered, and WSO, Capt Stanley M Imaye, downed a MiG-21 on the 29th of the month!

Ngu's kill was the only bright moment in a dark day for the VPAF, as a total of three MiG-21s were lost to the 366th TFW and 432nd TRW – two were claimed by the 432nd's Capt Steve Ritchie, leaving him just one short of becoming the USAF's sole pilot ace of the Vietnam War.

One of the MiG-21's lost on this day was a 921st machine that had been preparing to land at Noi Bai. Tailed by F-4s, the pilot had been instructed to divert to Kep. However, he misheard the order from his ground controller and ended up at Hoa Lac instead, where even more US fighters were swarming around. From there he was told to head for Gia Lam, but within minutes of receiving this transmission he was shot down.

The Vietnamese struck back on the 10th, when F-4J BuNo 155803 of VF-103 (embarked on the *Saratoga*) was destroyed by a MiG according to Navy records. No claim was made by the VPAF, however.

Another MiG-21 from the 921st fell victim to four F-4Ds from the 13th TFS/432nd TRW on 19 July. The pilot ejected, but was seriously injured when he landed in a tree. He died a few days later.

On the 24 July Nguyen Tien Sam and Ha Vinh Thanh registered kills once again, both pilots claiming to have destroyed a Phantom II apiece to the south-west of Hanoi – the USAF announced the loss of F-4E 66-0369 of the 421st TFS/366th TFW to an AAM, which had been fired by Sam. While they were preparing to land at Noi Bai, Thanh spotted a Phantom II behind him. And although he was just about to land, he opened the throttle and turned into his opponent, who chose not to continue with his attack. The MiG pilot then hastily touched down on the taxyway just as a second F-4 overflew him from the opposite direction! Nguyen Tien Sam, meanwhile had landed on the main runway.

That same day, Le Thanh Dao and Truong Ton from the 927th Fighter Regiment were involved in an engagement south of Hanoi. Dao

Also shot down on 27 June was F-4E 69-7271 again from the 366th TFW. Pilot Capt L A Aikman and WSO Capt Thomas J Hanton successfully ejected, and the former was rescued by a USAF SAR team. Hanton spent the rest of the war as a PoW, however (*VNA*)

MiG-21s await their next mission at Noi Bai in 1972. Aircraft 5015 stands out from the rest with its uniquely camouflaged uppersurfaces. This finish was achieved by simply overspraying the aircraft's bare metal exterior with irregular blotches of light and dark green paint. This aircraft may have been camouflaged prior to operating at remote VPAF airfields along the Laotian border. Note also the solitary MiG-21F-13 'Fishbed-C' (with its smaller fin and forward-hinged canopy) parked behind MiG-21PFM 5020 (*VNA*)

MiG-21PFM 5017 was also a recipient of the mottled green finish, although this became redundant when flying at night. Training to intercept night-flying B-52s, pilots relied heavily on the help of ground control radar during nocturnal sorties (*VNA*)

Six-kill ace Nguyen Tien Sam checks the guidance rollerons on an R-3S AAM that will soon be loaded beneath the wing of his 'Fishbed'. The Soviet-built missile was the staple weapon of the VPAF's MiG-21 force throughout the Vietnam War, the AAM having been developed in the USSR in 1960 as a direct copy of the American AIM-9B Sidewinder

chased an F-4 towards the sea and managed to shoot it down, while Truong Ton claimed another Phantom II – neither kill can be matched with American losses on the 24th. As the pilots were preparing to land at Kep, they spotted a section of F-4s approaching, so the pair flew on and recovered at Noi Bai under the protection of anti-aircraft artillery.

July ended with a spate of aerial engagements. On the 29th, the F-4D-equipped 13th TFS/432nd TRW and the F-4E-equipped 4th TFS/366th TFW each claimed a MiG-21. Ace Nguyen Tien Sam got one back that same day, however, when he destroyed F-4E 66-0367 of the 4th TFS/366th TFW, while fellow 927th ace Nguyen Duc Soat downed F-4D 66-7597 of the 523rd TFS/432nd TRW 24 hours later.

The month of August was to see the VPAF suffer more losses to both USAF and Navy F-4s, starting on the 10th when the crew of F-4J BuNo 157299 from VF-103 claimed a MiG-21. Two days later it was the turn of the 58th TFS/432nd TRW to claim a 'Fishbed', although this kill also had a naval connection, for the pilot of the F-4E was Marine Corps Capt Lawrence Richard and the WSO Navy Lt Cdr Michael Ettell, both men serving with the air force on exchange.

On the 15th a section of MiG-21s from the 921st, led by seven-kill ace Dang Ngoc Ngu, was bounced when radar units on the ground failed to warn them of enemy fighters nearby. Held for too long over Hung Yen before being vectored to Hoa Binh, two MiG-21s were downed over the latter airfield by F-4Es from the 336th TFS/8th TFW – only one claim was made by the Americans, however. Both MiG pilots were killed.

Four days later another MiG-21 was claimed by the crew of an F-4E from the 4th TFS/366th TFW, and on 28 August Capt Steve Ritchie, with Capt Charles DeBellevue as his WSO, downed his fifth MiG-21. DeBellevue would also become an ace the following month, finishing the conflict with six kills. Fellow 432nd TRW WSO Capt Jeffrey Feinstein would be the only other American ace of the war.

The sole VPAF success in August came on the 26th, when Nguyen Duc Soat downed Marine Corps F-4J BuNo 155811 of VMFA-232. This was the only land-based Marine Phantom II to be downed by a MiG during the Vietnam War.

The MiG-21 regiments enjoyed more successes in September. The 921st's Do Van Lanh, who for some undisclosed reason had been given the nickname 'Ironbird' earlier in the year (the name had previously been bestowed upon ace Nguyen Van Coc between 1965-68, although Lanh failed by a solitary kill to achieve 'acedom'), claimed an F-4E on the 9th, although the USAF credited this loss to a SAM. A single MiG-21 (and two MiG-19s) were in turn destroyed by the 555th TFS/432nd TRW.

Both sides 'traded punches' in mid-September, with the 927th's six-kill ace Le Thanh Dao downing F-4E 69-0288 of the 335th TFS/8th TFW on the 11th, and the crew of F-4J BuNo 155526 from VMFA-333 (embarked on the *America*) destroying a MiG-21. This was the sole MiG kill claimed by a Marine Corps squadron during the entire conflict, and this aircraft was lost to a SAM minutes after 'bagging' the VPAF fighter.

On the 12th it was the turn of 927th ace Nguyen Tien Sam to destroy a Phantom II, F-4E 69-7266, again from the 335th TFS/8th TFW, being destroyed by an AAM. The USAF fighter force quickly wreaked its revenge, however, with the 388th TFW claiming a trio of MiG-21s later that same day. The final MiG-21 kill in September came on the 16th, when the 555th TFS/432nd TRW claimed its 34th victory of the war.

More clashes occurred in October, with Nguyen Tien Sam downing F-4D 66-8738 of the 8th TFW on the 5th, and fellow 927th ace Nguyen Van Nghia destroying F-4E 69-7573 of the 307th TFS/432nd TRW 24 hours later. Losses were also suffered, however, with the 34th TFS/388th TFW claiming a MiG-21 on the 5th and a MiG-19 on the 6th. Two days later, it was the turn of the 388th's 35th TFS to claim a MiG-21.

The only other VPAF kill in October also involved the 388th TFW, for on the 12th Nguyen Duc Soat destroyed F-4E 69-0276 of the 34th TFS for his sixth, and last, kill. The remaining five fighters lost during the month were all MiG-21s, with the four units within the 432nd TRW each claiming a kill (on the 12th, 13th and two on the 15th) and the 34th TFS/388th TFW being credited with a solitary victory (also on the 15th).

On 22 October, President Nixon announced the suspension of bombing missions north of the 20th Parallel. Meanwhile, the level of US military aid being pumped into the South Vietnamese armed forces was dramatically increased, and new operations planned against the territories seized by the North Vietnamese Army during its Spring Offensive. B-52s continued to attack transport routes in the 4th Military District, and SR-71s flew reconnaissance missions north of the 20th Parallel. During this period, the badly mauled MiG-21 force succeeded in destroying just three Firebee drones.

And the lack of any real success against the mighty B-52 was not through any lack of trying on behalf of the VPAF. Senior officers had made meticulous studies of American tactics, and duly tried to devise counter-measures against the aircraft. However, nothing seemed to work.

For example, on 13 April 1972 B-52s attacked the airfield at Tho Xuan. A MiG-21 had scrambled but it failed to engage the bombers due to poor weather. Upon returning to base, the pilot found that conditions were so bad that he could not land, and he was forced to eject. Weeks later, a group of F-4s mimicking B-52 flight profiles and radio call-signs succeeded in fooling ground radar units. MiG-21s were scrambled to intercept a 'B-52', and one 'Fishbed' was duly shot down.

After several months of planning, the VPAF believed its tactics for dealing with the B-52s were at last ready as 1972 drew to a close. The stated intention was to shoot down a bomber and capture its pilots alive.

On 14 December, Nixon gave his approval for a plan to attack Hanoi and Hai Phong with B-52s in an effort to bring the North Vietnamese government back to the peace talks that they had stormed out of 24 hours earlier. The operation, known as *Linebacker II*, was set to start three days later. Several reconnaissance flights were made in advance over the target areas, and especially over surrounding airfields and air defence units.

On 17 December a class one alert was issued to Vietnamese units north of the 20th Parallel, and at 1940 hrs (Hanoi time) the following day, B-52s and fighter-bombers launched an attack on Kep, Noi Bai, Gia Lam, Hoa Lac and Yen Bai airfields, as well as the Dong Anh, Yen Vien and Duc Giang industrial centres and the North Vietnamese radio station at Me Tri. At the same time an attack was launched against Hai Phong.

As part of the *Linebacker II* campaign, F-111 aircraft were to fly in low to bomb the airfields, while F-4s would electronically target ground radar units and engage MiGs to the south-west along the Red River. B-52s were to approach Hanoi from the direction of Tam Dao, followed by 100 F-4s to keep the MiGs at bay. Four F-105G Wild Weasels were earmarked to attack radar units and SAM sites.

MiG-21MFs were kept on 24-hour alert at Noi Bai, Kep and Hoa Lac from 18 December, with pilots having to be ready to take off within six minutes of the alarm sounding during the day and seven minutes at night.

The radar unit at Quang Binh reported heavy jamming on the 18th. At 1830 hrs the 45th Radar Company, followed by the 16th Radar Company of the 291st Radar Regiment, detected a large number of B-52s heading north. At 1925 hrs three F-111s attacked Noi Bai. However, the runway remained operational, and Pham Tuan was ordered to take off;

'When flying over Hoa Binh, I saw a lot of chaff which came from F-4s, and also a considerable number of well-illuminated aircraft heading for Hanoi. I opened the throttle and tried to avoid the missiles fired at my aircraft. Soon I noticed another formation of aircraft, and switched on my RP-21 radar unit, but because of the jamming, I could not identify the targets. My presence did not go unnoticed by the Americans, and the B-52s increased their speed.'

That same night pilots were also ordered into the air from Hoa Lac, but they could not find the enemy. Although the MiG-21 units had failed to down a B-52 on the 18th, a gunner of one of the Boeing bombers (from the 307th SW) was credited with destroying a 'Fishbed' – there is no mention of this incident in VPAF records, however.

The B-52s kept up their attacks against Hanoi and Hai Phong during the following nights, and the North Vietnamese soon worked out the Americans' tactics. On the 23rd, the VPAF claimed to have downed four F-4s, but not a single loss was credited to MiG activity on this date by either the USAF or the Navy. The air force counter-claimed with MiG-21 kills on the 21st and 22nd (both by the 555th TFS/432nd TRW) and a second 'Fishbed' victory to the 307th SW on Christmas Eve.

Having failed to down a B-52, the VPAF decided to resort to drastic measures. Senior officers told pilots that if AAMs would not work, then a ramming attack was the only option left.

Despite ten days of solid bombing, every air base, with the exception of Noi Bai and Kep, remained operational. On 27 December a number of MiG-21s took off in an attempt to claim that elusive B-52. Among the pilots to get out of a patched up Noi Bai was Pham Tuan, who succeeded in recovering at Yen Bai with the help of ground control units situated in Moc Chau and Son La;

'At 2220 hrs I was given the order to take off from Yen Bai, and I broke through the low heavy cloud layer at 200-300 m, only to find F-4s in the vicinity. In the meantime, I was informed that the B-52s were approaching Moc Chau. The Son La and Moc Chau ground control units were constantly updating me on the distance of the bombers – 60 kilometres, 50 kilometres, 40 kilometres. As planned, I jettisoned my fuel tank and climbed to 7000 m. The radar units were plotting the route of the B-52s, and they also warned me of the escort of F-4s following the bombers.

'When I saw a yellow light in front of me, I increased my speed to 1200 km/h and climbed to an altitude of 10,000 m, where the B-52s were cruising. I radioed to the command, "I have the target in sight, request order for attack". The response was, "You have permission to fire twice, then escape quickly".

'The Americans were holding formation, keeping a separation of approximately two to three kilometres. I made last-minute checks on my missiles, and when I reached the level of the third B-52, I pushed the fire button on the control stick, launching two heat-seeking missiles from a distance of two kilometres. Huge flames were visible around the second B-52 as I broke sharply to the left and descended to 2000 m, before landing at Yen Bai. The attacked formation of B-52s immediately dropped their load and returned to base. The crew of the hit B-52 was killed.'

The loss of this bomber to MiG activity was never confirmed by the USAF, which instead claimed that the aircraft was struck by a SAM. The air force did, however, note the loss of two F-4Es from the 432nd TRW to AAMs, 67-0292 and 67-0234 being claimed by the same pilot, Tran Viet of the 921st – he was also credited with a third Phantom II kill on this date by the

A MiG-21UM 'Mongol-B' of the 921st Regiment departs on yet another training mission in the autumn of 1972, while MiG-21MFs are readied for the next round of missions against US fighter-bombers. MiG-21MF 5121 was used by Pham Tuan to 'down' a B-52D on the night of 27 December 1972 (*VNA*)

The wreckage of Pham Tuan's B-52D is picked over by villagers in a rice paddy on the outskirts of Hoa Binh on 28 December 1972. The USAF claimed that the mighty bomber was felled by a SAM (*VNA*)

VPAF. These were the last USAF F-4s downed by MiGs.

By the time the airfields at Noi Bai, Kep, Yen Bai and Gia Lam were attacked the following day, the VPAF had secretly flown all their MiG-21s to a brand new base at Cam Thuy, in Thanh Hoa province. Aside from this movement of airfields by the MiG regiments, the 28th also saw both the USAF (a 555th TFS/432nd TRW F-4D crew) and the Navy (F-4J BuNo 155846 from VF-142 off the *Enterprise*) claim single 'Fishbed' kills – this was the Navy's last MiG-21 victory of the war.

Pham Tuan (centre) explains how he shot down his B-52 to ace Nguyen Duc Soat (right). Tuan is dressed in a GS-6M helmet and green high-altitude flying suit – critical for the flights on which pilots intercepted B-52s, for the Boeing bombers would typically overfly the north at altitudes of up to 10,000 m. Soat and his unnamed colleague are wearing the standard attire of the day fighter pilot
(*Vietnamese Embassy, Budapest*)

Naval aviation did not escape unscathed on this day however, as a photo-recce RA-5C (BuNo 156633) of RVAH-13, again off the *Enterprise*, was listed by the Navy as having fallen victim to an AAM. There is no record of a claim against a Vigilante on this date within VPAF records, however. Nevertheless, this was the last loss attributed to a MiG to appear in official US listings for the conflict.

At 2141 hrs on the evening of the 28th, Vu Xuan Thieu took off from Cam Thuy and followed the B-52s with the help of ground control at Tho Xuan air base. He spotted the bombers over Son La, and even though he was very close, he launched a missile. One bomber exploded after being hit, and with Thieu unable to take avoiding action due to his proximity to his target, his MiG-21 disintegrated after being hit by debris. The following morning the wrecked aircraft were found lying close to one another. Again, the USAF stated that the B-52 was downed by a SAM.

On 30 December 1972, a suspension of the bombing campaign north of the 20th Parallel was announced. Both sides had returned to Paris for further talks about brokering a peace treaty.

Due to the state of Noi Bai air base, its MiG-21s had flown just 27 sorties between 18 and 30 December. The anti-B-52 campaign had achieved only modest results principally because only 13 out of 194 North Vietnamese fighter pilots had been trained for night-time operations.

Brig Gen Fesenko, who in 1972 was the main Russian adviser to the VPAF, kept a detailed record of the scores throughout the year, noting the following operational statistics. During 1972, the VPAF's fighter regiments had completed 823 missions (540 with MiG-21s, 207 with MiG-17s and 76 with MiG-19s) and had engaged US aircraft in 201 combats, claiming 89 of them shot down for the loss of 52 of their own (34 MiG-21s, nine MiG-17s and nine MiG-19s).

Every second Vietnamese pilot had less than 450 flight hours in his log-book. And in the autumn of 1972, of the 187 fighters assigned to the VPAF, only 47 were operational (31 MiG-21s and 16 MiG-17s). There are no records as to how many jets survived the *Linebacker II* raids, but most of them had been hidden away in bunkers, and only aircraft on alert remained at Noi Bai, Gia Lam, Yen Bai, Kep, Kien An and Tho Xuan.

The final loss suffered by the VPAF at the hands of American fighters occurred on 7 January 1973, when the crew of an F-4D from the 4th TFS/432nd TRW claimed a MiG-21 destroyed.

A NEW SPRING OFFENSIVE

The peace treaty was signed on 27 January 1973, and it stipulated that Vietnam was a sovereign country with its own territorial integrity. Washington agreed not to intervene in Vietnam, or in the internal affairs of the Vietnamese people, and that it would stop all military action against it, and call back all its forces from South Vietnam.

The VPAF had gone through immense changes since hostilities had begun. In 1965, it had only one fighter and one transport regiment. Eight years later, it was equipped with four fighter regiments, one transport regiment, and a training programme that trained 20 MiG-21 pilots at a time.

The technical support for these units had also changed drastically since the days in 1965 when the country had just two workshops to repair helicopters and MiG-17s. Ground control and command had also undergone sweeping changes.

The number of pilots and technical staff had increased, as had their skills. It had been important for the VPAF to hold its ground in an era when economic development was not possible, and when it depended on outside help both in terms of technical supply and training, and at the same time fight a numerically and technologically superior enemy.

The Communist Party hierarchy had given the VPAF the job of maintaining combat readiness, and defending North Vietnamese airspace, together with the Navy and the Air Defence Forces, against attack. However, it had been able to fulfil its tasks only in certain territories.

On 3 May 1973, the 927th 'Lam Son' Fighter Regiment was transferred to Tho Xuan and merged with the unit already serving there. At the end of the year, some fighter and bomber regiments were put under the control of the 371st 'Thang Long' Air Division, which had its headquarters at Gia Lam. The bases at Kep, Yen Bai, Kien An, Tho Xuan, Vinh, Anh Son and Dong Hoi came under the control of a different unit.

The 927th Fighter Regiment was moved to Kep, while the 921st remained at Noi Bai. In January 1974, in line with the strategy to defend the north while supporting the fighting in the south, VPAF commanders gave the job of protecting the airspace above Routes 1 and 3, near Hanoi, to the 921st. It was also told to be prepared to relocate to Vinh and Dong Hoi if the need arose. The 927th was to defend the areas north-east and south-east of Hanoi, and be able to move to Tho Xuan if necessary.

After the *Linebacker II* campaign, the VPAF had sent 42 MiG-21 pilots to the Soviet Union for further bad weather and night training – a second group undertook similar training in February 1974. At home, 34 out of 185 trainee pilots were also night-qualified. However, the number of night-capable jets available was limited to just one for every ten pilots.

Following the lessons learned from continued fighting in the south during 1973 and 1974, the Communist Party's political committee met between October and December 1974 to discuss the situation. It decided that South Vietnam would have to be 'liberated' between 1975 and 1976, so the 927th Fighter Regiment was duly relocated to Noi Bai, leaving only a few construction units at Kep.

Sat in a KM-1 ejection seat fitted into a MiG-21PFM 'Fishbed-F', this unidentified North Vietnamese pilot wears a ZS-3 helmet with a blue-tinted visor over a black SL-60 (summer version) leather helmet. The last four digits (8610) of the MiG's serial number can be seen stencilled on the inside of the canopy framing immediately above the pilot's head. The optical ASP-PF-21 gunsight, fixed to the windscreen framing, is also clearly visible (*Vietnamese Embassy, Budapest*)

The Southern Liberation Campaign started on 4 March 1975, with the first attack at Tay Nguyen, in the central highlands. Soon, Buon Ma Thuot was captured, and the central highlands taken. The airfields at Buon Ma Thuot and Play Cu were also captured, as well as equipment abandoned by South Vietnamese forces.

On 25 March Hué fell, together with the air base at Phu Bai and the radar unit at Thuan An. The North Vietnamese immediately transferred two air defence regiments and two SAM battalions to Hué. Four days later, Da Nang was taken, along with the air base. At about the same time the radar unit on Son Tra peninsula was also captured.

The VPAF was also involved in the invasion, although the intention was to keep the MiGs' missions secret, even from the Russian technical officers serving in the north – the Vietnamese government did not want Russian pilots in-country fighting the western-backed South Vietnamese, thus turning the conflict into another Korean War. However, it was difficult, if not impossible, to keep these missions a secret, for MiG-21s were taking off fully armed with bombs and rockets and returning without them. Meanwhile, the faces of the VPAF pilots spoke volumes about the missions they were flying.

Sometimes groups of four or five Russian technical personnel would be taken by helicopter to small forward bases with earth landing strips to repair battle-damaged MiG-21s. They were not told where they were, and they were not allowed to speak to the locals. Sometimes, the airstrips would be attacked by South Vietnamese aircraft, but by the end of May 1975 the battles were over, and the Russian personnel were allowed to return to Noi Bai.

Two months after the end of the Vietnam War, some of the VPAF pilots faced a new challenge. The younger ones stayed in the north, but the older, more experienced ones moved to the south to form new fighter regiments flying captured American aircraft.

AIRFIELDS AND MAINTENANCE

Direct attacks by the Americans on North Vietnamese airfields were sporadic in 1966, although they become more regular from April the following year once these bases had been removed from the restricted list by the US government. The busiest months were May, October and November of 1967, and February 1968.

By the summer of 1967 six airfields were deemed suitable for fast jet operations – Noi Bai, Gia Lam, Kep, Hoa Lac, Kien An and Tho Xuan.

As part of a drive for air force success, senior VPAF officers had decided that a North Vietnamese fighter should be in the air at all times, and to achieve this, a taxiway at Noi Bai was also used as its runway. This presented a problem for the pilots due to its short length, but at the same time it gave them an advantage, for they were able to surprise their enemy. Indeed, according to American intelligence, Noi Bai did not possess a second runway long enough to facilitate MiG-21 operations.

No fewer than 50 missions were flown from the taxiway, with aircraft using SPRD-99 rocket-assist take-off (RATO) bottles to get airborne. Unable to land on Noi Bai's bomb-damaged main runway, pilots either ejected after the mission, or recovered at another airfield.

In October 1967 the Americans revised their tactics. All efforts would now be concentrated on paralysing VPAF operations, using the so-called 'in the nest' principle – hitting aircraft on the ground at their bases. Kien An, Cat Bi and Gia Lam were attacked again and again, as were Hoa Lac (33 times), Kep (29 times), Kien An (25 times) and Noi Bai (nine times).

At Noi Bai, Nguyen Huu Tu, Vu Van Dinh and Pham Duy Sinh – officers in the construction unit – searched for American time-delay bombs in order to disarm them. Nguyen Van Hoanh and Hoang Hai, (two young soldiers from the 921st Fighter Regiment) did the same thing, personally disarming no fewer than 60 bombs and removing 4000 anti-personnel mines scattered all over the base.

Villagers from Kim Anh and Da Phuc also joined in the repair effort at the airfield, helping to get rid of the mines as well. Ten members of the local militia would search the

This North Vietnamese MiG-21MF 'Fishbed-J' is seen taking off from one of Noi Bai's taxiways with the assistance of two SPRD-99 take-off booster rockets during anti-*Linebacker* operations in mid-1972. The spent rocket pods would be jettisoned soon after take off (*VPAF Museum*)

Groundcrew perform routine maintenance out in the open on a MiG-21F-13 'Fishbed-C' from the 921st Regiment in 1967 (*Tran Dinh Kiem*)

Simple earth blast pens were hastily built in 1967-68 to protect aircraft at Noi Bai, Kep, Kien An and Gia Lam. Here, technicians from the 921st manhandle a MiG-21PFM 'Fishbed-F' back into its pen at Kep (*VPAF Museum*)

base, followed 200 m behind by village girls who filled in bomb craters if any ordnance happened to go off.

At this time Noa Bai looked like a building site, with everyone working to get it back into action. Only one radar unit remained active (and even that was five kilometres away) to provide assistance for military action. Secondary back-up radar sites were situated between five and ten kilometres away, while additional coverage was provided by sites even further afield. Contact between units was maintained with radio, telephone and by courier.

Following the attacks, bases relocated their storage facilities to appropriate shelters more than ten kilometres away, and petrol and jet fuel was trucked in depending on requirements at the time, instead of being stored on-site. Meanwhile, engineers Bui Thanh Tiem, Pham Hoa Lan, Nguyen Trong Cat and Vu Quoc Dat tried to work out how best fighter regiments could operate despite all this disruption.

Noi Bai had to evacuated after the fifth attack in 1967, but still the Americans returned – six times in November and seven in December. Sometimes, repairs were done in an amazingly short time, the base at Kep, for example, being restored to operational status in just one night (on 24 October 1967) thanks to the efforts of local civilians and the army. Similar feats occured at Kien An following an attack on 17 November, which had seemingly destroyed its runways. These were reopened in just two days following non-stop repair work by the 28th Technical Brigade.

In the course of American air raids against Noi Bai, Kep, Kien An and Hoa Lac between January 1967 and March 1968, seventeen aircraft, three helicopters and numerous fuel trucks, buildings and runways were destroyed. In 50 per cent of the raids, the target airfield would be put out

of action from as little as five hours to several days. Of all the bombs dropped, about 40 per cent found their mark, with 30 per cent hitting runways and ten per cent taxyways. In all, these four bases were put out of action on 36 separate occasions, for a total of 120 days over a period of 15 months.

Due to the increasing number of attacks on airfields, the government agreed to a request from the Ministry of Defence and the VPAF that individual provinces should be ordered to repair damaged bases.

In order to speed up the repair of airfields, 70,000 reinforced concrete plates were manufactured and stored just a kilometre from the various bases. The plates were made in two sizes – 1.8 x 1.8 m, with a thickness of 20 cms, and 1 x 1 m, with a thickness of 16 cm. And thousands of tonnes of earth was moved from Dong Giao, Dong Mo, Trai Hut and Xuan Hoa to Gia Lam, Kien An, Kep, Yen Bai, Noi Bai and Hoa Lac for use in repairs and camouflaging.

Preparations for airfield repair took the equivalent of 200,000 working days to complete, 70 per cent of which were carried out by civilians. Earth shelters were built for the fighters on the airfields, as well as at the foot of surrounding hills, while underground command and control centres were also constructed, along with shelters for technical equipment.

Groundcrewmen overhaul the hydraulic system fitted in the detachable tail section of a MiG-21MF 'Fishbed-J' (*VPAF Museum*)

The aircraft shelters were usually positioned between 500 and 2000 m from the runway, although sometimes they were sited as far away as 3000 m. The concrete taxyways from the shelters were 20 m wide, and could also serve as runways. Jet fuel storage tanks were placed underground about 200 m apart.

Following the first raids in the wake of this construction work, it became readily apparent that the earth shelters provided protection against standard high-explosive bombs, but not against other types of ordnance.

New shelters were duly constructed in their place. They looked like normal huts, although their roofs were made from rails and the steel plates used for runway construction, with 20-25 cm of soil then piled on top and covered with turf. The structure was based on the dimensions of the MiG-21, being 15 m long, 10 m wide and 7 m high, and using up 30-35 rails and 300 plates (each 4 m long). Smaller MiG-17s were never housed in the revised shelters.

With no airfield cleaning machinery being made available to the VPAF throughout the conflict, regiments had to resort to using a small army of soldiers and civilians equipped with straw brooms to keep the runways and taxyways clear of dirt and debris following raids. This staged shot, taken at Noi Bai, also shows MiG-21PF 'Fishbed-D' 4227 parked in its revetment. All three 'sweepers' are wearing helmets, so perhaps the base was expecting another attack at some point in the near future (*VPAF Museum*)

A partially-fuelled MiG-21PFM is flown into Noi Bai in 1968, slung beneath a Mil Mi-6. A special harness was designed for the underslung aircraft, with two softly-lined straps being wrapped around the fuselage and then attached to a trapeze. Three cables from the hook of the Mi-6 were also connected to the trapeze, while two others were attached to the wingtips. 'Fishbeds' had to be airlifted into Noi Bai during the early war years because the main runway at the base was too short for the MiG-21's long landing roll out (*VPAF Museum*)

As a variation on the theme, some airfields boasted earth shelters resembling sheds, with steel plates being used instead of rails. These were 18 m long, 14 m wide at the base and 6 m high. The steel plates in the roof were riveted together. In all, some 450 plates measuring 4 m and 200 measuring 2 m were needed for each shed – a total of 140 aircraft and 200 truck shelters were built. Aside from these permanent structures, literally hundreds of bamboo rods and bales of straw were also used to protect the aircraft against shrapnel from fragmentation bombs.

Senior officers ordered that much of this building work be camouflaged, so a 2-3 cm thick layer of soil that blended in with the surrounding area was placed on top of new buildings, runways and taxyways.

Later, aircraft were also hidden in the villages – in Kim Da, in Vinh Phu province, thousands of trees were planted to hide the MiGs. Civilians readily gave up their homes and barns for the military to live in, and to use as storage areas for armament and fuel.

VPAF fighters would also be transported beneath Mi-6 helicopters to mountain caves up to 30 kilometres away, where they were then pushed into their hiding places by truck. A special harness was designed to protect the aircraft, with two softly-lined straps being thrown around the fuselage and attached to a trapeze. Three cables of 12 mm thickness were then connected from the hook of the Mi-6 to the trapeze, while two others were attached to the wingtips. The Mi-6 was able to lift a fully-fuelled and armed MiG-17, but in the case of MiG-19s and MiG-21s, only empty aircraft could be carried.

Ground defences around all airfields were also drastically improved, with AAA and SAM sites proliferating. The three most heavily defended bases were Noi Bai, Gia Lam and Kien An, each of which was protected by seven 100 mm AAA batteries, four 57 mm AAA batteries, BTR-40 mobile flak platforms and an SA-2 SAM regiment. The 923rd and 925th Fighter Regiments also had their own air defence battalions, equipped with 37 mm batteries, protecting Kep and Yen Bai.

After Tho Xuan air base was completed in 1968, MiGs would patrol the southern front from here while the bombed-out airfields at Vinh, Dong Hoi, Anh Son and Gat were rebuilt.

As part of the construction programme of the late 1960s, a runway was built at Phu Quy to accommodate transport aircraft, while bases at Na San and Dien Bien, as well as those in Laos at Xam Nua, Canh Dong Chum and Xepon, were reinforced and restored to operational status. And finally, airfields at Tho Xuan, Vinh, Do Luong, Anh Son and Dong Hoi were equipped with new communication systems, and back-up runways were added.

From the end of 1968, the North Vietnamese made the most of the lull provided by the Americans. By May of the following year, however, Noi Bai was still scarred by at least 230 bomb craters, Gia Lam by 204, Kep by 222, Kien An by 114 and Tho Xuan by 30. Rebuilding work took time and energy, and while each airfield would have needed 80 specialist engineers to carry out the work, only 148 were available for the entire base network. Unskilled civilian labour still had a part to play. Indeed, the bases at Hoa Lac, Mieu Mon, Tho Xuan, Anh Son and Dong Hoi were all rebuilt with civilian help in 1969-70, and

Equipped with two underwing tanks and R-3S missiles, this MiG-21MF 'Fishbed-J' was photographed by a USAF RF-4C during a photo-reconnaissance mission over Gia Lam in 1972. The fighter is sat in front of a cleverly camouflaged hut-shaped shelter of the type constructed after the raids of 1967-68 had revealed the need for improved revetments (*via István Toperczer*)

peasants constructed additional landing strips in the villages of Cam Thuy, Gat and Phu Quy.

As an example of civilian workers in action, between May and July 1969, soldiers of the 28th Technical Brigade, helped by locals, worked day and night at Vinh. The runway was repaired and 174 bomb craters were filled in. The villages surrounding the airfields across Vietnam would provide a 'defensive circle', keeping a ready supply of raw materials on hand for quick repairs after each attack.

The provision of electrical power to VPAF bases also proved problematic, with the principal sites at Gia Lam and Noi Bai enjoying a good supply of electricity, while most other airfields had to rely on generators.

Ground support centres were also upgraded as the war progressed, with most control towers being modified to house new equipment capable of operating in all weathers. Eventually, there were eight communication and control centres stretching all the way from Tho Xuan to Quang Binh, named B1 through to B8. To make the command and control system more effective, the units at Noi Bai were put under the direct command of the 923rd Fighter Regiment at Kep, the 925th Fighter Regiment at Yen Bai and the 919th Air Transport Regiment at Gia Lam.

THE LAST ACT

Following the instigation of Operation *Linebacker I* on 10 May 1972, the Americans launched sustained attacks against VPAF air bases, specifically targeting runways and suspected aircraft shelters and storage areas. The air force, believing that this new campaign would last for some time, and that it would increase in ferocity, made some quick base changes.

VPAF HQ was relocated from Gia Lam to Ngoc Dong, while the former base was allocated to the 921st Fighter Regiment for both fighter and transport aircraft. A command unit was set up at Dong Hoi at the same time, and the one in Quang Binh province was moved to Tho Xuan.

Military planners were concerned about fuel supplies for the aircraft, following the mining of Hai Phong harbour. No fuel could get through by sea, so all supplies were having to come overland by train, and the earliest this would arrive was November. Jet fuel stored at Noi Bai was therefore distributed to a variety of different locations as a safety precaution – Gia Lam was one such site, receiving 250 tons of fuel.

Despite the ferociousness of *Linebacker I*, the units responsible for rebuilding damaged airfields and repairing aircraft received new equipment, and specialists. Even new airfields were built, including Tan Trai and Dien Trach.

The raids continued, however, and on 17 December 1972, a class one alert was ordered for Vietnamese units north of the 20th Parallel. At 1940 hrs (Hanoi time) the following day, Operation *Linebacker II* was launched, with B-52s and fighter-bombers striking Kep, Noi Bai, Gia Lam, Hoa Lac and Yen Bai. While

A pilot and his crewchief monitor the engine start of their MiG-21PFM (*VPAF Museum*)

the soldiers turned their attention to defending the bases from further attacks, the civilian population set about rebuilding the airfields – with the exception of Noi Bai and Kep, every base remained operational.

Between the 22nd and the 26th, F-111s regularly visited Yen Bai, and the southern, eastern and northern ends of the airfield were completely destroyed. By the time Noi Bai, Kep, Yen Bai and Gia Lam were attacked again on 28 December, the VPAF had secretly flown all of its serviceable MiG-21s to the new base at Cam Thuy, in Thanh Hoa province.

Armament technicians check the starboard R-3S AAM fitted to a 927th Regiment MiG-21PFM 'Fishbed-F', while an airframe specialist inspects work carried out on the tailplane and jetpipe of a MiG-21MF (*VPAF Museum*)

On 30 December 1972, bombing north of the 20th Parallel was suspended by the Americans and *Linebacker II* came to an end. The VPAF's airfields had been badly damaged, with bases to the south of Thanh Hoa being completely out of order, and the runways at Noi Bai, Kep, Yen Bai and Kien An having been left in a dreadful state by the bombing attacks.

To allow the VPAF to regain its strength over the next three years, considerable effort was made to repair these key bases, and other sites, using both military and civilian labour. As part of this work, more than 10,000 cubic metres of earth was moved to fill in craters at Tho Xuan, Vinh, Anh Son, Dong Hoi, Ta Con, Na San, Cam Binh, Tan Trai, Phu Tho and Cam Thuy.

This work continued on well into the mid-1970s, and was still underway when, on 30 April 1975, soldiers of the People's Army of Vietnam marched into Saigon from five different directions. By 1130 hrs the North

Mechanics from the 12th Company of the 927th Regiment prepare to tow a recently-landed MiG-21PFM back to its revetment. The fighter lacks missiles on its underwing rails, so perhaps its most recent flight was purely a training mission. If the MiG had seen action, its pilot would have jettisoned his centreline tank prior to engaging the enemy (*VPAF Museum*)

Vietnamese flag was flying over the Presidential Palace, signalling the end to the Ho Chi Minh campaign. The first VPAF aircraft with North Vietnamese national markings landed at Tan Son Nhut on 1 May 1975, and on 15 May Ton Duc Thang and other senior political leaders arrived in Saigon on board a VPAF Il-18 to celebrate the victory.

Within hours of VPAF aircraft landing at Tan Son Nhut, 27 ex-South Vietnamese pilots had volunteered for service with the communists. Dubbed 'new recruits' by the North Vietnamese, they would be followed by many others. Four ex-American transport aircraft were quickly restored to flying condition, and scheduled flights commenced between Hanoi and Saigon, and from Saigon to the southern provinces. Control tower equipment was also repaired and put back into operation, as were a further 54 aircraft. On 22 May, a report was sent to VPAF command detailing the airfields and aircraft that had been seized.

The size of Vietnamese airspace increased with reunification, and to boost the strength of the VPAF, southern airfields were brought under its control. These included Phu Bai, Da Nang, Nha Trang, Phan Rang, Phu Cat, Play Cu, Bien Hoa, Tan Son Nhat, Can Tho and Da Lat. By the end of 1975, the take-over was complete, and every airfield operational.

MiG MAINTENANCE & SOVIET SPONSORS

In May 1972, Vietnamese technical units were working day and night inspecting and repairing existing MiG-21MF (Type 96) 'Fishbed-J' aircraft for the 921st Fighter Regiment, as well as assembling new ones.

Technicians also devised several innovations that helped to extend the service life of the aircraft, while maintenance units concentrated on repairing battle and accident damage.

Apart from the North Vietnamese groundcrews, so called 'advisers' – specialists from friendly countries – were also playing an active part in Vietnam's war. The Chinese helped at bases where Chinese-built aircraft operated, while small groups of up to 30 Russian technicians (engineers, propulsion system technicians and airframe, armament and radio specialists) were working at Noi Bai and Kep on MiG-21s, and enjoying a very restricted freedom of movement.

The 'Fishbeds' were shipped to Vietnam by sea, where they were assembled by Soviet engineers and test flown by Soviet pilots. The fact that the latter flew the jets in-theatre has led to speculation in the west over the years that these same men also took part in active service. The Vietnamese flatly deny this, for at the time they were keen to avoid any direct confrontation between the superpowers. It is true that in 1964-65, two or three North Korean pilots were serving at Gia Lam, but they had returned home long before the war broke out.

However, on 11 November 1972 an accidental air combat incident

A veteran Soviet flight instructor explains basic dogfighting techniques with the aid of model 'Fishbeds' to North Vietnamese pilots in the spring of 1975. Behind him is the almost mandatory communist icon of the father of Soviet socialism, Vladimir Lenin (*Zoltán Pintér*)

involving a foreign national took place that resulted in a raw recruit seeing action a little earlier than he expected. A North Vietnamese student pilot and his Soviet instructor were practising dogfighting manoeuvres in an unarmed MiG-21 'Mongol' two-seat trainer, when they were informed by ground control that four F-4 Phantom IIs were just eight kilometres from their base, and flying in their direction at low altitude!

Despite the defenceless MiG having just 800 litres of fuel left in its tanks, the crew were ordered to get out of the area, but before they could do so a pair of Phantom IIs broke away from the attack formation and climbed to higher altitude to cut off any possible escape. The remaining pair went after the MiG.

Assuming control of the jet, the Russian pilot initally tried to escape by flying a tight turn in full afterburner. In the ensuing seconds, he and his student spotted AIM-9 Sidewinders coming for them, so they performed more defensive manoeuvres. The missiles failed to hit, and exploded when their programmed self-destruct mechanisms kicked in.

Thanks to ground control units, the MiG crew were kept fully informed about what the Americans were up to. Four more missiles were launched at them, and as if the situation was not bad enough, the tight 50-80 m turns that the instructor was having to make on full reheat in order to evade the missiles were rapidly using up the 'Mongol's' fuel.

In the end, the MiG drained its tanks faster than the F-4s used up their missiles, and with only 100 litres of fuel left, the Soviet instructor had no choice but to get out of the MiG along with his student. He started to climb. Within 500 m the engine stopped, just as another attack was launched. A missile hit the MiG's rear fuselage, but the crew ejected safely – no kill claims were made by either the USAF or the Navy on this day.

The Soviet technicians' main role was to teach the Vietnamese everything they needed to know about how to work and maintain the MiG-21. However, it was up to the Vietnamese as to whether they listened

Russian technicians show their North Vietnamese counterparts how to assemble a newly-arrived MiG-21. This scene was repeated literally hundreds of times over during a decade of war in Vietnam

to this advice or not. For instance, the Russians could not stop the VPAF from using an aircraft on which servicing had not been finished. The air force was keen to get as many aircraft reassembled and passed through the hands of the Russian technicians as quickly as possible, since they were certain that the MiGs were in perfectly good shape for frontline service.

Most North Vietnamese pilots spoke good Russian after years of training at Krasnodar, in the Soviet Union, as did some of the mechanics. However, in most cases an interpreter was required, which led to numerous misunderstandings.

The North Vietnamese made the most of Russian generosity, accepting every aircraft and weapon offered. When the number of available aircraft outnumbered the pilots available to fly them, the older examples were put into long-term storage. This provided a decent reserve for use during the American raids of 1972.

This strategy did not always work, however. For example, in early 1972 20 surplus MiG-21PF 'Fishbed-Ds' were parked neatly in a row within a four-kilometre-long taxiway that had been dug into a cave near the runway at Noi Bai. During preparations for the 1975 offensive, these aircraft were checked for possible use, and while they had all survived American attacks unscratched in their secure 'bunker', three years in a humid environment without proper care had rendered them completely useless. They were so corroded that not even an overhaul back in the Soviet Union would have saved them. Besides the aircraft, a considerable number of spare parts for earlier types were also hidden away in the cave, and these too proved to be unusable.

Further problems were revealed during the American bombing campaign in 1972 when the MiG-17s' sole maintenance factory was hit. Training units, deprived of aircraft, had to move to China. This helped

Senior military officers and communist party members tour an exhibition of weapons and aircraft that were put on display at Noi Bai in 1970. MiG-21PF 'Fishbed-D' 4326 was the aircraft used by ranking VPAF ace Nguyen Van Coc to down at least one of the nine kills he claimed between 1967 and 1969. The surface-to-air missiles positioned behind the MiG are both SA-2 'Guidelines' – North Vietnam's principal SAM system throughout the conflict (*VPAF Museum*)

bring about a rethink on the storage policy for surplus jets, and once the peace treaty had been signed, the VPAF decided that all aircraft kept in safe shelters should be immediately returned to airfields and re-commissioned. Maintenance units worked day and night putting together 26 aircraft of various types. By November 1973, the duties of the 919th Air Transport Corps included the reassembly of new fighters at Cat Bi.

On 22 February 1974, the North Vietnamese and Chinese governments agreed a deal between their two air forces, under which Chinese help was promised in setting up a new maintenance factory for MiG-17s.

This camouflaged MiG-21MF 'Fishbed-J' carries a single AAM and a FAB-250 bomb beneath its starboard wing. It was photographed upon its return from a mission over South Vietnam during the spring invasion of 1975 (*VPAF Museum*)

During the offensive of 1975, North Vietnamese forces pushing southward captured one air base after another after they had been abandoned by the retreating South Vietnamese forces. Each airfield was packed with aircraft, for the Saigon regime's fleet of modern types, and support equipment, had been one of the most powerful in South-east Asia.

The two aircraft repair facilities, at Tan Son Nhut and Bien Hoa, were particularly rich prizes, for they both boasted 59 workshops each, plus a considerable number of smaller support units of various sizes spread over 282 airfields. The maintenance and repair facility at Bien Hoa was taken over on 31 May and converted into a helicopter repair facility, while the damaged transport aircraft repair site at Tan Son Nhut was rebuilt.

Abandoned F-5s and A-37s were also soon requisitioned, while newly-acquired helicopters and transport aircraft fell under the supervision of the 919th Air Transport Corps. Ground personnel took over the storage facilities, workshops and air traffic control equipment.

By the end of 1975, 877 aircraft had been seized, although only 20 per cent of these were operational. At Tan Son Nhut, a host of transports and military aircraft were now in North Vietnamese hands, including 23 A-37s, 41 F-5s, 50 UH-1s, five AD-6s, five CH-47s and five U-6As. Also requisitioned were 15 U-17s, 41 L-19s, 28 C-7As, 36 C-119s, 18 T-41s, 21 C-47s, seven C-130s, seven DC-3s, five DC-4s and two DC-6s.

In July, the airfields at Binh Tuy and Lo Te were put back into service, along with a further 117 aircraft. From here, fighting continued against islands in the Southern Sea and along the Cambodian border.

At Tan Son Nhut, the 919th Air Transport Corps repaired 97 aircraft to satisfy transport requirements, while at Bien Hoa an additional 83 machines were restored to airworthiness, and a further 39 at Da Nang. The transport aircraft repair facility at Tan Son Nhut repaired 34 transport and reconnaissance aircraft, while the unit at Bien Hoa had nine fighters ready and 27 spare engines.

The Soviet Union was offered a considerable amount of the captured American-built equipment, and in November 1975 Russian specialists arrived at Da Nang to take their pick of the more interesting types. They

Above and below
In the wake of the 'liberation' of South Vietnam in 1975, the fighter regiments at Noi Bai participated in a victory parade that was attended by senior VPAF officers and communist party officials (*VPAF Museum*)

took one F-5E with full technical documentation and all its spare parts, along with two additional engines in factory condition and ground support equipment. The available A-37s were also checked out, and the one in best condition was chosen, along with back-up equipment. An AC-119 was also offered, but because of the problems the aircraft's size posed when it came to transporting it by sea, only the gunship's internal equipment was considered worthwhile for scrutiny back in the USSR.

Apart from the fighters, a CH-47 and a UH-1 were also loaded on board a Russian ship. Some other friendly communist countries also received a few American aircraft for further research.

EPILOGUE

The air war between US and VPAF aircraft took place in three periods – from 1965 to 1968, from 1969 to 1971 and throughout 1972 and into the first two weeks of 1973. Fighter combat was played out at speeds between mach 0.5 to 1.0, and at altitudes between 150 and 9000 m.

The outcome depended on many things – the pilots' level of training, the hardware available, the efficiency of ground control units, the flying and tactical characteristics of the aircraft, and the actual tactics employed. Since the Americans were at a considerable advantage in terms of training, number of aircraft in-theatre and command and control, the North

Vietnamese had to use the virtues of the surprise attack, trying to avoid open confrontation whenever they could.

There were victories and blunders on both sides, but the official kill and loss ratio shows a considerable difference between the air arms. According to the official US Navy study, sponsored by the Chief of Naval Operations, that identified the probable causes for all in-flight combat losses during the Vietnam War, 91 aircraft were shot down (or probably shot down) in air-to-air encounters – six of these fell to Chinese fighters after straying into China's airspace. In return, US aircraft were credited with shooting down 193 VPAF machines and at least one Chinese fighter.

The North Vietnamese fighter force claims to have shot down 320 aircraft, while admitting the loss of only 134 of its own. It is interesting to note that the Americans admitted the loss of 22 aircraft that are not even mentioned in North Vietnamese reports, but that there were 64 US losses that match exactly on both sides.

A lot more time is needed for the precise details of every aerial engagement to be researched, and for the fate of all the participants to be brought to light. At the moment, Vietnam's jungles, rice fields and sea still hold the remains of almost 550 American airmen, as they do also those of an indeterminate number of North Vietnamese pilots.

The reasons for the VPAF losses can be attributed to many causes. The most common mistakes made by pilots were hasty decisions at the outset of aerial engagements, improper use of weapon systems, poor flying skills, especially in holding formation and over-confidence when breaking off a dogfight. It is true that with experience most of these failings were ironed out, only for the next generation of young pilots to repeat them.

Apart from the faults of the pilots, there were serious problems in the command centres, such as in making a correct assessment of the situation in the air during battle, giving wrong instructions to pilots and making mistakes in directing fighters to their target. All these factors added to the losses. Many pilots had to endure hair-raising moments because of flawed information given out by fighter controllers on the ground, where the aerial encounters were being plotted on tables and maps.

Due to the time it took for information to be absorbed by control room staff, plotted and new orders given, the pilots usually got their target co-ordinates much too late. Often, the symbols for different multi-aircraft strike forces were mixed up by the operators, and by the time they had got themselves out of the muddle, the pilots would again be getting old information.

Radar was another problem. When the dots of the interceptors and of the attacking US aircraft merged on a radar screen during an encounter, the directional outcome would often depend on the level of training and expertise of the operator. Furthermore, fighters were often lost because the pilots were not given permission for individual action when they had been directed to a target. The control structure was rigid, and orders had to be obeyed.

Another factor was the constant introduction of new tactics by the Americans, to which the North Vietnamese could not always devise a suitable reply in time. Much of this forced VPAF pilots to make independent decisions in the heat of battle. Based on their experience, they would lay down the following basic rules for themselves;

In the years following the war school children would often visit the 931st Air Division at Yen Bai. This particular MiG-21bis was one of a number of 'Fishbed L/Ns' supplied to the VPAF from 1979. These pilots are each holding a white ZS-5 helmet (with light blue, dark green or dark brown visors) in their hands (*VPAF Museum*)

An ex-South Vietnamese F-5A taxies past MiG-21MFs at Bien Hoa in the late 1970s. The 935th Fighter Regiment of the 372nd Air Division (established on 30 May 1975) was a unique unit within the VPAF, for its pilots flew both MiG-21s and F-5A/Es from Bien Hoa (*VNA*)

'1.) If you come across a pair or flight of enemy aircraft, try to find where their escorts are before deciding how to attack.

'2.) Always look for new possibilities and avoid stereotypical solutions in a dogfight.

'3.) The enemy can discover us only after we have completed our attack.'

A successful fight was defined by spotting the enemy as early as possible, identifying their battle strategy, approaching them unseen, using the weapon system correctly and remaining vigilant up to the very last moment of taxying and shutting down the engine.

Hundreds of aerial engagements took place between the first clash in April 1965 and the last in January 1973, but they provided the USAF, the US Navy and Marine Corps, the Vietnamese and other communist countries flying MiGs with an unprecedented wealth of tactical experience to be used in training future generations of pilots.

APPENDICES

APPENDIX A

NOSE (BORT) NUMBERS OF NORTH VIETNAMESE MiG-21s

MiG-21PF	MiG-21F-13	MiG-21?	MiG-21PFM	MiG-21MF	MiG-21PFM
4120-4129	4420-4429	*4620-4629*	5001-5009	5101-5109	6120-6129
4220-4229	4520-4529		5010-5019	5110-5119	*6130-6139?*
4320-4329			5020-5029	5120-5129	6140-6149
			5030-5039	5130-5139	
			5040-5049	5140-5149	
			5050-5059	5150-5159	
			5060-5069		
			5070-5079		

Numbers in italics are not confirmed

APPENDIX B

MiG-21 ACES OF THE VPAF

Name	Victories	VPAF aircraft	Regiment	Service
Nguyen Van Coc	Nine kills	MiG-21	921st	1967-69
Pham Thanh Ngan	Eight kills	MiG-21	921st	1967-69
Nguyen Hong Nhi	Eight kills	MiG-21	921st/927th	1966-72
Mai Van Cuong	Eight kills	MiG-21	921st	1966-68
Dang Ngoc Ngu	Seven kills	MiG-21	921st	1966-72
Vu Ngoc Dinh	Six kills	MiG-21	921st	1966-70
Nguyen Ngoc Do	Six kills	MiG-21	921st	1967-68
Nguyen Nhat Chieu	Six kills	MiG-17/21	921st	1965-67
Le Thanh Dao	Six kills	MiG-21	927th	1971-72
Nguyen Dang Kinh	Six kills	MiG-21	921st	1967-68
Nguyen Duc Soat	Six kills	MiG-21	921st/927th	1969-72
Nguyen Tien Sam	Six kills	MiG-21	921st/927th	1968-72
Nguyen Van Nghia	Five kills	MiG-21	927th	1972

APPENDIX C

MiG-21 PILOTS AND UNITS OFFICIALLY HONOURED AS HEROES

Nguyen Hong Nhi	June 1969	921st 'Sao Do'	22 Dec 1969
Nguyen Van Coc	June 1969	921st, 1st Squadron	Dec 1966 and Aug 1970
Pham Thanh Ngan	June 1969	921st, 3rd Squadron	18 Jun 1969 and 11 Jan 1973
Mai Van Cuong	December 1969	927th 'Lam Son'	20 Dec 1973
Vu Ngoc Dinh	August 1970	927th, 9th Squadron	31 Dec 1973
Nguyen Ngoc Do	August 1970		
Dang Ngoc Ngu	January 1973		
Do Van Lanh	January 1973		
Le Thanh Dao	January 1973		
Nguyen Duc Soat	January 1973		
Nguyen Tien Sam	January 1973		
Pham Tuan	September 1973		
Nguyen Van Nghia	September 1973		
Nguyen Nhat Chieu	December 1973		
Dinh Ton	December 1973		
Truong Khanh Chau	December 1973		

APPENDIX D

MiG-21 AERIAL VICTORIES

Date	Location	US Aircraft	US Crew	VPAF Aircraft	Regiment	Vietnamese Aircrew
04 Mar 66	Quang Ninh	Firebee	-	MiG-21	921	Nguyen Hong Nhi
05 Mar 66	unknown	Firebee	-	MiG-21	921	unknown
07 Jun 66	unknown	F-105D	Bayles	MiG-21	921	unknown
09 Jun 66	unknown	F-4		MiG-21	921	unknown
09 Jun 66	unknown	F-4		MiG-21	921	unknown
07 Jul 66	**Tam Dao**	**F-105D**	**Tomes**	**MiG-21**	**921**	**Tran Ngoc Xiu**
11 Jul 66	**Son Duong**	**F-105D**	**McClelland**	**MiG-21**	**921**	**Vu Ngoc Dinh**
						Dong Van Song
21 Sep 66	unknown	F-105D	Ammon	MiG-21	921	unknown
05 Oct 66	*unknown*	*F-4C*	*Garland, Andrews*	*MiG-21*	*921*	*unknown*
09 Oct 66	unknown	F-4B	Tanner, Terry	MiG-21	921	Nguyen Van Minh
09 Oct 66	unknown	F-4		MiG-21	921	Nguyen Van Minh
02 Dec 66	Noi Bai	F-4C	Burns, Ducat	MiG-21	921	unknown
02 Dec 66	Noi Bai	F-4C	Flesher, Berger	MiG-21	921	unknown
05 Dec 66	**unknown**	**F-105D**	**Begley**	**MiG-21**	**921**	**unknown**
05 Dec 66	unknown	F-105 or F-4		MiG-21	921	unknown
08 Dec 66	unknown	F-105D	Asire	MiG-21	921	unknown
08 Dec 66	unknown	F-105D		MiG-21	921	unknown
14 Dec 66	**unknown**	**F-105D**	**Cooley**	**MiG-21**	**921**	**Dong Van De**
14 Dec 66	unknown	F-105D		MiG-21	921	unknown
14 Dec 66	unknown	F-105D		MiG-21	921	unknown
28 Apr 67	*unknown*	*F-105*	*D Caras*	*MiG-21*	*921*	*unknown*
30 Apr 67	**Vinh Phu**	**F-105D**	**R Abbott**	**MiG-21**	**921**	**Nguyen Ngoc Do**
30 Apr 67	**Vinh Phu**	**F-105D**	**J Abbott**	**MiG-21**	**921**	**Nguyen Van Coc**
30 Apr 67	**unknown**	**F-105F**	**Thorness, Johnson**	**MiG-21**	**921**	**Le Trong Huyen**
30 Apr 67	unknown	F-105		MiG-21	921	Vu Ngoc Dinh
12 May 67	Van Yen	F-105F	Pitman, Stewart	MiG-21	921	Le Trong Huyen
						Dong Van Song
22 May 67	Hanoi	F-4C	Perrine, Backus	MiG-21	921	Dang Ngoc Ngu
11 Jul 67	Hai Duong	A-4		MiG-21	921	Le Trong Huyen
						Dong Van Song
17 Jul 67	Lang Chanh	F-8		MiG-21	921	Nguyen Nhat Chieu
20 Jul 67	Nho Quan	F-4		MiG-21	921	Nguyen Ngoc Do
						Pham Thanh Ngan
26 Jul 67	unknown	RF-4C	Corbitt, Bare	MiG-21	921	unknown
10 Aug 67	unknown	RF-4C	Lengyel, Myers	MiG-21	921	unknown
23 Aug 67	Nghia Lo	F-105D	Baker	MiG-21	921	Nguyen Nhat Chieu
23 Aug 67	**Nghia Lo**	**F-4D**	**Tyler, Sittner**	**MiG-21**	**921**	**Nguyen Van Coc**
16 Sept 67	**Son La**	**RF-101C**	**Bagley**	**MiG-21**	**921**	**Nguyen Ngoc Do**
16 Sept 67	Son La	RF-101C	Patterson	MiG-21	921	Pham Thanh Ngan
17 Sept 67	unknown	RF-4C	Venanzi, Stavast	MiG-21	921	unknown
03 Oct 67	*unknown*	*F-4D*	*Moore, Gulbrandson*	*MiG-21*	*921*	*unknown*
07 Oct 67	**Ha Bac**	**F-105F**	**Howard, Shamblee**	**MiG-21**	**921**	**Nguyen Van Coc**
09 Oct 67	*unknown*	*F-105D*	*Clements*	*MiG-21*	*921*	*unknown*
08 Nov 67	**Hanoi**	**F-4D**	**Gordon Brenneman**	**MiG-21**	**921**	**Nguyen Hong Nhi**
08 Nov 67	Hanoi	F-4		MiG-21	921	Nguyen Dang Kinh
?? Nov 67	unknown	F-4		MiG-21	921	Nguyen Van Coc
18 Nov 67	**Phuc Yen**	**F-105F**	**Dardeau, Lehnhoff**	**MiG-21**	**921**	**Nguyen Van Coc**
18 Nov 67	**Phuc Yen**	**F-105D**	**Reed**	**MiG-21**	**921**	**unknown**
19 Nov 67	unknown	EB-66		MiG-21	921	Vu Ngoc Dinh
						Nguyen Dang Kinh
20 Nov 67	*unknown*	*F-105D*	*Butler*	*MiG-21*	*921*	*unknown*
12 Dec 67	Son Dong	F-105		MiG-21	921	unknown
16 Dec 67	*unknown*	*F-4D*	*Low, Hill*	*MiG-21*	*921*	*unknown*
17 Dec 67	**unknown**	**F-105D**	**Ellis**	**MiG-21**	**921**	**Vu Ngoc Dinh**
17 Dec 67	unknown	F-105		MiG-21	921	Vu Ngoc Dinh
17 Dec 67	unknown	F-105		MiG-21	921	Nguyen Hong Nhi
19 Dec 67	Tam Dao	F-105		MiG-21	921	Nguyen Van Coc
19 Dec 67	Tam Dao	unknown		MiG-17 or -21	921	unknown
19 Dec 67	Tam Dao	unknown		MiG-17 or -21	921	unknown
19 Dec 67	Tam Dao	unknown.		MiG-17 or -21	921	unknown

Date	Location	Aircraft	Crew	MiG	Unit	Pilot
03 Jan 68	**Thanh Son**	**F-105D**	**Bean**	**MiG-21**	**921**	**Nguyen Dang Kinh**
03 Jan 68	Thanh Son	F-105		MiG-21	921	Bui Duc Nhu
03 Jan 68	Yen Chau	F-105		MiG-21	921	Ha Van Chuc
14 Jan 68	**Hoi Xuan**	**EB-66C**	**Mercer, Terrell+5**	**MiG-21**	**921**	**Nguyen Dang Kinh** **Dong Van Song**
14 Jan 68	*Yen Bai*	*F-105D*	*Horne*	*MiG-21*	*921*	*unknown*
18 Jan 68	*unknown*	*F-4D*	*Simonet, Smith*	*unknown*	*unknown*	*unknown*
18 Jan 68	*unknown*	*F-4D*	*Hinckley, Jones*	*unknown*	*unknown*	*unknown*
03 Feb 68	**unknown**	**F-102A**	**Wiggins**	**MiG-21**	**921**	**Nguyen Van Coc**
04 Feb 68	*Thai Nguyen*	*F-105D*	*Lasiter*	*MiG-21*	*921*	*unknown*
23 Feb 68	*unknown*	*F-4D*	*Guttersen, Donald*	*MiG-21*	*921*	*unknown*
03 Mar 68	unknown	EB-66		MiG-21	921	Nguyen Dang Kinh Nguyen Duc Thuan
07 May 68	**Do Luong**	**F-4B**	**Christensen, Kramer**	**MiG-21**	**921**	**Nguyen Van Coc**
16 Jun 68	**Do Luong**	**F-4J**	**Wilber, Rupinski**	**MiG-21**	**921**	**Dinh Ton**
01 Aug 68	Do Luong	F-8		MiG-21	921	Nguyen Hong Nhi
19 Sept 68	unknown	F-8C		MiG-21	921	unknown
21 Sept 68	unknown	Firebee		MiG-21	921	Nguyen Dang Kinh
26 Oct 68	Dien Chau	F-4		MiG-21	921	unknown
?? Dec 69	unknown	Firebee		MiG-21	921	Nguyen Van Coc
?? Dec 69	unknown	Firebee		MiG-21	921	Nguyen Van Coc
18 Jan 70	Vinh	F-4		MiG-21	921	Phan Dinh Tuan
28 Jan 70	**Vinh**	**HH-53B**	**Bell, Leeser +4**	**MiG-21**	**921**	**Vu Ngoc Dinh**
20 Nov 71	unknown	B-52 damaged		MiG-21	921	Vu Dinh Rang
18 Dec 71	**unknown**	**F-4D**	**Johnson, Vaughan**	**MiG-21**	**921**	**Le Thanh Dao**
18 Dec 71	**unknown**	**F-4D**	**Stanley, O'Brien**	**MiG-21**	**921**	**Vo Si Giap**
27 Apr 72	**Vu Ban**	**F-4B**	**Molinare, Souder**	**MiG-21**	**921**	**Hoang Quoc Dung**
10 May 72	Kep	F-4		MiG-21	921	Dang Ngoc Ngu
10 May 72	Tuyen Quang	F-4		MiG-21	921	unknown
10 May 72	Hai Duong	F-4J	Blackburn, Rudloff	MiG-21	927	Le Thanh Dao
10 May 72	Hai Duong	F-4J	Cunningham, Driscoll	MiG-21	927	Vu Duc Hop
11 May 72	**Hanoi**	**F-4D**	**Kittinger, Reich**	**MiG-21**	**927**	**Ngo Van Phu**
11 May 72	**Hanoi**	**F-105G**	**Talley, Padgett**	**MiG-21**	**927**	**Ngo Duy Thu**
18 May 72	Kep	F-4		MiG-21	927	Nguyen Hong Nhi
20 May 72	**Suoi Rut, Phu Ly**	**F-4D**	**Markle, Williams**	**MiG-21**	**921**	**Do Van Lanh**
23 May 72	Nam Dinh	F-4D	Byrns, Bean	MiG-21	921	unknown
23 May 72	*unknown*	*A-7B*	*Barnett*	*MiG-21*	*927*	*Nguyen Duc Soat*
24 May 72	*unknown*	*F-8J*	*Beeler*	*unknown*	*unknown*	*unknown*
01 Jun 72	Suoi Rut, Viet Tri	F-4E	Hawks, Dingee	MiG-21	921	Pham Phu Thai
10 Jun 72	unknown	unknown		MiG-21	921	unknown
13 Jun 72	**Vinh Phu**	**F-4E**	**Hanson, Fulton**	**MiG-21**	**921**	**Pham Phu Thai**
13 Jun 72	Vinh Phu	F-4		MiG-21	921	Do Van Lanh
21 Jun 72	**unknown**	**F-4E**	**Rose, Callaghan**	**MiG-21**	**921**	**Do Van Lanh**
24 Jun 72	**Thanh Son**	**F-4E**	**Grant, Beekman**	**MiG-21**	**927**	**Nguyen Duc Soat**
24 Jun 72	Thanh Son	F-4		MiG-21	927	Ngo Duy Thu
24 Jun 72	**Thanh Son**	**F-4D**	**McCarty, Jackson**	**MiG-21**	**927**	**Nguyen Van Nghia**
26 Jun 72	unknown	F-4		MiG-21	921	unknown
27 Jun 72	Noa Binh	F-4		MiG-21	927	Ngo Duy Thu
27 Jun 72	unknown	F-4E	Sullivan, Francis	MiG-21	921	Nguyen Duc Nhu
27 Jun 72	**Hoa Binh**	**F-4E**	**Cerak, Dingee**	**MiG-21**	**927**	**Nguyen Duc Soat**
27 Jun 72	**Nghia Lo**	**F-4E**	**Aikman, Hanton**	**MiG-21**	**921**	**Pham Phu Thai**
27 Jun 72	**Nghia Lo**	**F-4E**	**Miller, McDow**	**MiG-21**	**921**	**Bui Thanh Liem**
05 Jul 72	**Ha Bac**	**F-4E**	**Spencer, Seek**	**MiG-21**	**927**	**Nguyen Tien Sam**
05 Jul 72	**Ha Bac**	**F-4E**	**Elander, Logan**	**MiG-21**	**927**	**Ha Vinh Thanh**
08 Jul 72	**unknown**	**F-4E**	**Ross, Imaye**	**MiG-21**	**921**	**Dang Ngoc Ngu**
10 Jul 72	*unknown*	*F-4J*	*Randall, Masterson*	*MiG-17 or -21*	*unknown*	*unknown*
24 Jul 72	**Hanoi**	**F-4E**	**?/?**	**MiG-21**	**927**	**Nguyen Tien Sam**
24 Jul 72	Hanoi	F-4		MiG-21	927	Ha Vinh Thanh
24 Jul 72	Hanoi	F-4		MiG-21	927	Le Thanh Dao
24 Jul 72	Hanoi	F-4		MiG-21	927	Truong Ton
29 Jul 72	**unknown**	**F-4E**	**Kula, Matsui**	**MiG-21**	**927**	**Nguyen Tien Sam**
30 Jul 72	**unknown**	**F-4D**	**Brooks, McAdams**	**MiG-21**	**927**	**Nguyen Duc Soat**
26 Aug 72	**unknown**	**F-4J**	**Cordova, Borders**	**MiG-21**	**927**	**Nguyen Duc Soat**
09 Sept 72	unknown	F-4E	Dalecky, Murphy	MiG-21	921	Do Van Lanh
11 Sept 72	**unknown**	**F-4E**	**Ratzlaff, Heeren**	**MiG-21**	**927**	**Le Thanh Dao**
12 Sept 72	**Lang Son**	**F-4E**	**McMurray, Zuberbuhler**	**MiG-21**	**927**	**Nguyen Tien Sam**
05 Oct 72	**unknown**	**F-4D**	**Lewis, Alpers**	**MiG-21**	**927**	**Nguyen Tien Sam**
06 Oct 72	**unknown**	**F-4E**	**Anderson, Latella**	**MiG-21**	**927**	**Nguyen Van Nghia**

12 Oct 72	**Hanoi**	**F-4E**	**Young, Brunson**	**MiG-21**	**927**	**Nguyen Duc Soat**
23 Dec 72	unknown	F-4		MiG-21	921	unknown
23 Dec 72	unknown	F-4		MiG-21	921	unknown
23 Dec 72	unknown	F-4		MiG-21	921	unknown
23 Dec 72	unknown	F-4		MiG-21	921	unknown
27 Dec 72	Hoa Binh	B-52D		MiG-21	921	Pham Tuan
27 Dec 72	**unknown**	**F-4E**	**Jeffcoat, Trimble**	**MiG-21**	**921**	**Tran Viet**
27 Dec 72	**unknown**	**F-4E**	**Anderson, Ward**	**MiG-21**	**921**	**Tran Viet**
27 Dec 72	unknown	F-4E		MiG-21	921	Tran Viet
28 Dec 72	*unknown*	*RA-5C*	*Agnew, Haifley*	*MiG-21*	*921*	*unknown*
28 Dec 72	Son La	B-52D	Lewis +6	MiG-21	921	Vu Xuan Thieu

Key

Vietnamese source
US source
Vietnamese source corresponding to US source

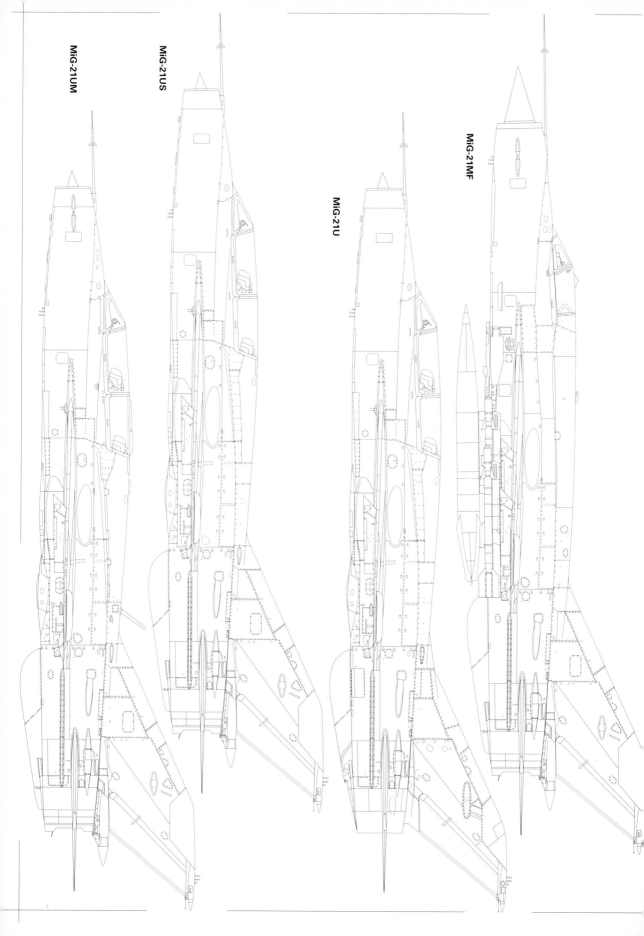

MiG-21UM

MiG-21US

MiG-21U

MiG-21MF

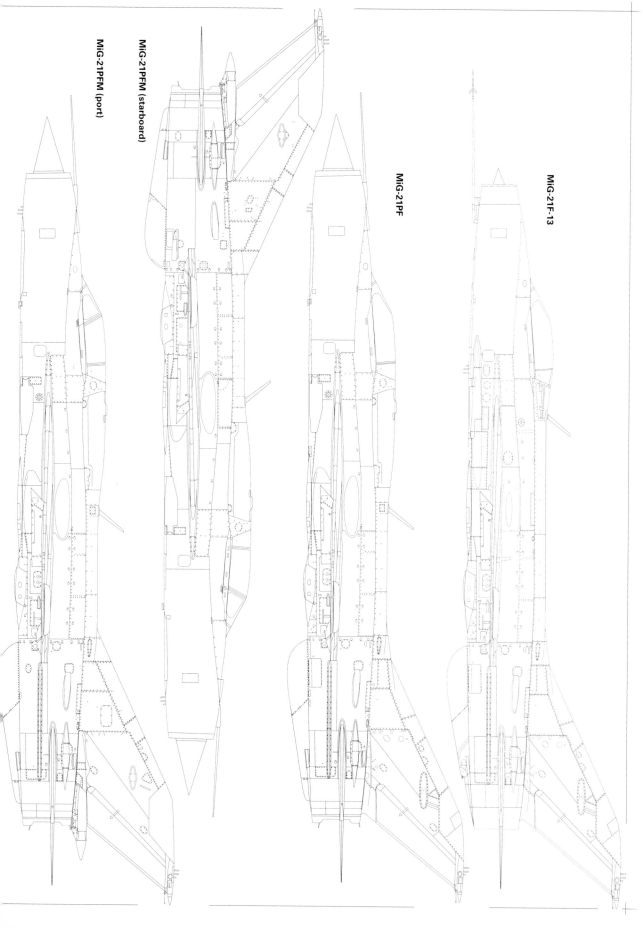

MiG-21PFM (port)

MiG-21PFM (starboard)

MiG-21PF

MiG-21F-13

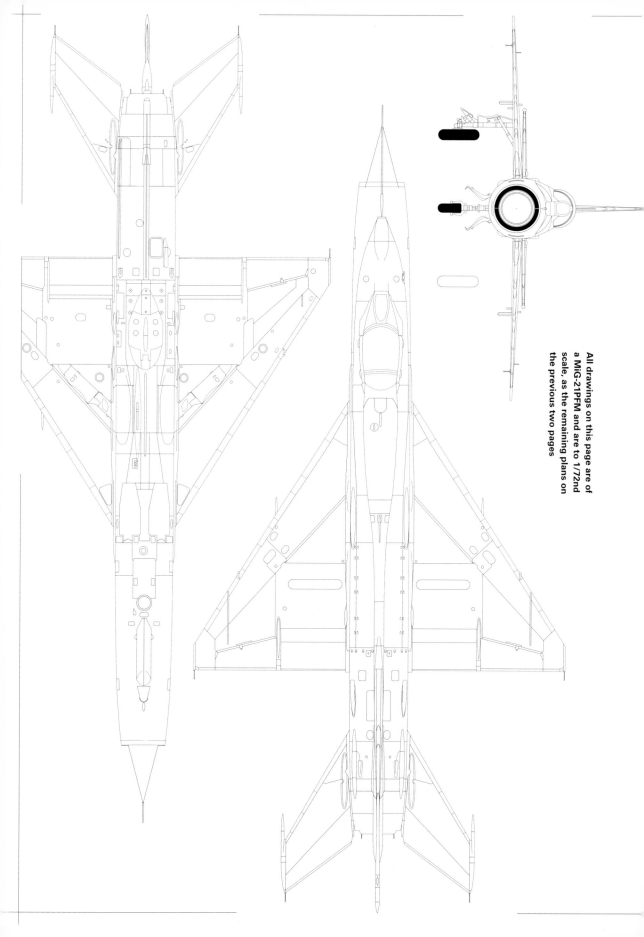

All drawings on this page are of a MiG-21PFM and are to 1/72nd scale, as the remaining plans on the previous two pages

COLOUR PLATES

1 & 2
MiG-21F-13 'Fishbed-C' 4420 of Nguyen Ngoc Do and MiG-21F-13 'Fishbed C' 4520 of Pham Thanh Ngan, both from the 921st 'Sao Do', 16 September 1967

On 16 September 1967, two USAF reconnaissance aircraft were claimed shot down by VPAF MiG-21F-13s over Son La. Nguyen Ngoc Do used 4420 to destroy Maj B R Bagley's RF-101C (56-0180 of the 20th TRS/432nd TRW), while Pham Thanh Ngan was flying 4520 when he downed Capt R E Patterson's RF-101C (56-0181, from the same unit). The USAF admitted the loss of Bagley's jet to MiG activity, but listed Patterson's aircraft as having been shot down by a SAM.

3
MiG-21PF 'Fishbed-D' 4128 of 921st 'Sao Do', April 1966

This 'Fishbed', which was used by the 921st Fighter Regiment from Noi Bai, arrived in Vietnam in April 1966 with the first batch of MiG-21PF variants. The Moscow-based Znamya Truda factory produced the PFV (V for Vietnam) variant specially for the VPAF, this aircraft effectively being a 'tropicalised' MiG-21PF. One of the principal changes made to Vietnamese 'Fishbeds' was the replacement of the RP-21 radar with the improved, and more robust, R-2L unit.

4
MiG-21PF 'Fishbed-D' 4324 of Nguyen Dang Kinh, 921st 'Sao Do', 19 November 1967

This MiG-21PF enjoyed success with no less than nine different pilots whilst serving with the 921st Fighter Regiment in 1967-68, these individuals claiming a total of 14 kills between them from November 1967 through to May 1968. One of the first to enjoy success in 4324 was future six-kill ace Nguyen Dang Kinh, who 'shared' in the destruction of an EB-66 on 19 November 1967 with fellow six-kill ace Vu Ngoc Dinh. The USAF failed to list an EB-66 lost on this day, however.

5
MiG-21PF 'Fishbed-D' 4326 of Nguyen Van Coc, 921st 'Sao Do', 7 May 1968

Photographs of MiG-21PF 4326 displaying 13 kill markings appeared in numerous western publications in the late 1960s, and this tally was credited to the fictitious VPAF ace 'Colonel Tomb' or 'Toon' – the victory stars actually denoted the combined tallies of several pilots that had flown the jet in 1967-68. In fact, the real Vietnamese 'ace of aces', Capt Nguyen Van Coc, had used this 'Fishbed' to down Lt Cdr E S Christensen and Lt(jg) W A Kramer's F-4B Phantom II BuNo 151485 (from VF-92, embarked on board the *Enterprise*) over Do Luong on 7 May 1968. Coc would eventually be credited with the destruction of nine US aircraft between 1967 and 1969.

6
MiG-21PFM 'Fishbed-F' 5015 of the 921st 'Sao Do', 1972

This MiG-21PFM of the 'Sao Do' Fighter Regiment was given a one-off mottled dark green camouflage scheme. The hand-sprayed finish was applied to the fighter's uppersurfaces, which had first been painted an overall shade of light green. The MiG's undersides remained natural metal. Such schemes were applied in an effort to prevent US reconnaissance aircraft detecting VPAF 'Fishbeds' operating from southern bases.

7
MiG-21PFM 'Fishbed-F' 5020 of Nguyen Tien Sam, 927th 'Lam Son', 5 July 1972

This MiG fighter, bearing 12 kill markings, was flown at various times by 927th Regiment aces Le Thanh Dao, Nguyen Duc Soat and Nguyen Van Nghia during anti-*Linebacker* missions in 1972. On 5 July, fellow ace Nguyen Tien Sam used it to destroy Capt W A Spencer and 1Lt B J Seek's F-4E 67-0296 (of the 34th TFS/388th TFW) with a single AAM over Ha Bac. He fired the round at very close range to ensure that the missile tracked, and when the Phantom II exploded, Sam was forced to fly through the blast, which temporarily stalled the engine of his fighter. Fortunately, the veteran MiG-21PFM restarted, and Sam managed to cover his wingman, Ha Vinh Thanh, as he shot down a second F-4E (67-0339) from the 34th TFS/388th TFW.

8
MiG-21PFM 'Fishbed-F' 5033 of Tran Viet, 921st 'Sao Do', 27 December 1972

This 'Fishbed' was used by the 921st's Tran Viet to claim the final two victories of the Vietnam conflict that can be verified by official US loss listings. On 27 December he was credited by the VPAF with the destruction of three Phantom IIs, although USAF records note that only the F-4Es of Maj C H Jeffcoat and 1Lt J R Trimble (67-0292) and Capt J W Anderson and 1Lt B H Ward (67-0234) were lost to MiG activity. Both crews hailed from the 13th TFS/432nd TRW. The identity of the third F-4E remains unknown.

9
MiG-21PFM 'Fishbed-F' 5040 of Le Thanh Dao, 927th 'Lam Son', 10 May 1972

On 10 May 1972, Le Thanh Dao and wingman Vu Duc Hop scrambled in their MiG-21PFMs (Dao's was painted in an overall dark green camouflage scheme) and intercepted an incoming Navy strike package heading for a target west of Hai Phong. As section leader, Dao got to fire first, and at a distance of 1500 m he triggered an AAM. According to his post-mission report, the missile struck an F-4J, which crashed at Hai Duong. At the controls of the Navy fighter (BuNo 155797) were VF-92's

XO, Cdr Harry L 'Habu' Blackburn, and RIO Lt Steve A 'Sar' Rudloff, the pair having launched off the *Constellation*. Captured after ejecting from their blazing fighter, the crew stated upon their repatriation the following year that their F-4J had suffered a direct hit over the target area from a solitary 85 mm AAA round. And this is how the loss of BuNo 155797 is officially recorded by the Navy.

10
MiG-21PFM 'Fishbed-F' 5066 of the 927th 'Lam Son', 1972
5066 also served with the 927th 'Lam Son' in 1972, being one of the handful of 'Fishbeds' oversprayed with softly-dappled camouflage of dark green over natural metal. One of the last PFMs delivered to the VPAF, it had initially served with the 921st in an unpainted state.

11
MiG-21PFM 'Fishbed-F' 6122 of the 927th 'Lam Son', 1972
Hastily delivered to the VPAF as an attrition replacement in 1969, this ex-Soviet Air Forces MiG-21PFM 'Fishbed-F' arrived in Vietnam already camouflaged in a standard Warsaw Pact scheme. The only changes made by its new owners prior to the fighter being rushed into service were the addition of a North Vietnamese Bort number in red and the replacement of the Soviet national marking with the VPAF 'star and bar'. The number '6' in the Bort serial noted that this machine was one in a series of MiG-21PFMs shipped to North Vietnam, along with Shenyang J-6s (MiG-19Ss), in 1969. Following the 'Liberation' of South Vietnam in 1975, all surviving MiG-21PFMs were handed over to the 372nd Air Division at Da Nang.

12
MiG-21PFM 'Fishbed-F' (no Bort number) of the 921st 'Sao Do', 1972
During the early 1970s the Soviet Air Forces and several Warsaw Pact countries began to paint their MiG-21MFs and bis variants in a variety of schemes. Included amongst the latter was East Germany, which repainted a small number of its older MiG-21PFMs. This overall grey jet was one such machine, arriving at the 921st from East Germany as an attrition replacement. Lacking a VPAF Bort number, the only way Vietnamese pilots and groundcrews could identify these aircraft was by the last four digits of the serial number which were painted onto the left side of the pitot tube and inside the canopy framing.

13
MiG-21PFM 'Fishbed-F' 5026 of the 927th 'Lam Son', 1972
Typical of the many ex-Soviet Air Forces 'Fishbed-Fs' that were rushed to the VPAF following the heavy fighting of 1968, this machine remains totally devoid of any distinguishing unit markings or personal emblems.

14
MiG-21MF 'Fishbed-J' 5117 of Truong Ton, 927th 'Lam Son', 24 July 1972
This 'Fishbed-J' was flown by the 927th's Truong Ton during a sprawling dogfight fought over Hanoi on 24 July 1972. He and flight-leader Le Thanh Dao each claimed an F-4 shot down, although the USAF admitted the loss of just one Phantom II to MiG activity on this day – pilots from the 927th were credited with four kills by the VPAF! The 927th's Kep base was badly bombed whilst this aerial battle was taking place over the North Vietnamese capital, and all four pilots had to divert to Noi Bai.

15
MiG-21MF 'Fishbed-J' 5121 of Pham Tuan, 921st 'Sao Do', 27 December 1972
MiG-21MF 5121 displays eight kill markings on its nose, these almost certainly being the aircraft's accumulated score in the hands of several pilots. Its regiment, the 921st 'Sao Do', was credited with 137 aerial victories by the VPAF during the conflict in Vietnam. One of those kills was claimed by Capt Pham Tuan in 5121 on the night of 27 December 1972, when he 'shot down' a B-52D over Hoa Binh – the USAF is adamant that none of its Boeing bombers were downed by MiGs, those being lost falling to SAMs or AAA. On 23 July 1980, Pham Tuan became a Vietnamese cosmonaut when he and Russian Viktor Vasiliyevich Gorbatko launched into space aboard Soyuz-37. They remained in orbit for 79 days.

16
MiG-21U 'Mongol-A' 4124 of the 921st 'Sao Do', 1968
The first trainer version of the 'Fishbed' retained the overall dimensions of the MiG-21F-13, with the export variant of the MiG-21U (Type 66) being built at the Znamya Truda facility in Moscow between 1964 and 1968. One of the first air forces to receive examples of the two-seat 'Mongol', the VPAF ushered the MiG-21U into service at Noi Bai in late 1965, ahead of receiving its first MiG-21F-13 single-seaters.

17
MiG-21US 'Mongol-B' 5046 of the 921st 'Sao Do', 1969
The second generation MiG-21 trainer was similar to the MiG-21PF/PFM family, and aircraft were built at Tbilisi between 1966 and 1970. This particular MiG-21US (Type 68) is armed with UB-16-57 rocket pods in anticipation of a live firing training exercise.

18
MiG-21UM 'Mongol-B' 5903 of the 927th 'Lam Son', 1972
The MiG-21UM (Type 69) was the third generation of 'Fishbed' trainer to see service with the VPAF. The 'Mongol-B' was improved through the fitment of new equipment and avionics, and built from

1971 in Tbilisi. As with previous 'Mongol' variants, the instructor pilot in the rear cockpit was equipped with a retractable periscope for use during take-off and landing. The VPAF still possesses a considerable fleet of MiG-21UMs, which it employs as its principal lead-in trainer for pilots destined to fly the 150+ MiG-21bis that entered service with the air force between 1979 and 1984. Despite its age, the 'Fishbed' is still very much the staple fighter of today's VPAF, examples serving with six regiments and the Air Force Academy.

Back Cover
MiG-21PFM 'Fishbed F' 5006 of the 921st 'Sao Do', February 1972

When the Hungarian prime minister visited the 921st and 927th Fighter Regiments in 1972, this particular MiG-21PFM was serving in the Sao Do ('Red Star') regiment. On the basis of its nose number, this aircraft was amongst the first batch of nine PFMs built for the VPAF in the MiG factory in Moscow in 1966 – the final examples of the 79 on order were delivered in late 1968. In 1967 a number of 'used' PFMs also arrived from East Germany as emergency attrition replacements. The MiG-21PFM was not equipped with an internal gun, although it was possible to mount a GP-9 gun pod on the centreline pylon of the ex-East German aircraft in place of the external fuel tank – such a fit significantly reduced the fighter's range, however. The North Vietnamese PFMs were not delivered with the correct wiring to allow the GP-9 pod to be fitted, although this technical oversight was subsequently rectified.

COLOUR SECTION

1 & 2
The Thai Nguyen Military District museum houses eight-kill ace Pham Thanh Ngan's MiG-21F-13 'Fishbed-C', which was formerly coded 4520

3
MiG-21PF 'Fishbed-D' 4326 (serial number 8511) displays 13 kill markings. It belongs to the Air Defence Museum at the Vietnamese People's Air Force Headquarters at Bach Mai airfield, Hanoi

4
MiG-21PF 'Fishbed-D' 4324 also features kill markings that denote the success that pilots achieved whilst flying it in combat. The veteran fighter is displayed at the People's Army Museum in Hanoi

5
Six-kill ace Nguyen Tien Sam's MiG-21PFM 'Fishbed-F' 5020 from the 927th 'Lam Son' Fighter Regiment displays 12 victory markings. The fighter has resided in Hanoi for many years

6
A close-up of the nose of 5020, this jet being sat on a concrete block alongside MiG-21MF 5121

7
Capt Pham Tuan was flying MiG-21MF 'Fishbed-J' 5121 on the night of 27 December 1972 when he claimed a B-52 shot down over Hoa Binh

8
A close-up of the 'star-spangled' nose of Tuan's 'Fishbed-J' 5121

9
This European Theatre-camouflaged ex-Soviet Air Forces MiG-21PFM 'Fishbed-F' resides within the Da Nang air base museum

10
In the cockpit of this MiG-21PFM 'Fishbed-F', the circular screen for the RP-21 radar can be seen level with the pilot's head. It was used to search and track aerial targets in bad weather, at night and from long distances. The radar's primary role was to guide the RS-2US (K-5) air-to-air missile until impact (*via Z Pintér*)

11
The dismembered remnants of a handful of discarded MiG-21PFMs and MFs, as well as several MiG-17Fs, are seen slowly decaying in a forgotten corner of Phu Cat air base

12
MiG-21UM 'Mongol-B' 8107 served for many years as a trainer with the 921st Fighter Regiment, and is today preserved in the Nha Trang air base museum

13
As one of the first batch of VPAF MiG-21MF 'Fishbed-Js' delivered, 5108 (serial number 4908) is also preserved at the museum at Nha Trang

14 & 15
Although not strictly from the Vietnam War period, being delivered to the VPAF in 1979, MiG-21bis 'Fishbed-L' 5236 (serial number 75076118) has nevertheless now been retired just like its famous forbears and put on display in Hanoi's Lenin Square. Painted in two shades of grey, the aircraft saw active service with the 921st Fighter Regiment at Noi Bai

16
The armament of North Vietnamese MiG-21s included first generation AAMs from the 1950s. The RS-2US (NATO codename AA-1 'Alkali', or K-5) radio-command guided air-to-air missile had a devastating effect with its blast-fragmentation warhead. It weighed 82.3 kg, was 2.5 m long and had a 200 mm diameter. The 'Alkali' could be launched from a distance of 2500 to 5200 m from the target, at altitudes of between 2500 and 20,500 m. It possessed a maximum speed of 2340 km/h. The passive infra-red homing version of the K-5 was designated the K-55. The missile enjoyed little success in combat over Vietnam

93

17

The AAM of choice within the VPAF, the R-3S (western name K-13 'Atoll') infra-red homing missile was a direct copy of the American AIM-9B Sidewinder. The weapon was 2.8 m long, with a diameter of 127 mm. It weighed 75.3 kg, and had a blast-fragmentation warhead. The R-3S could be launched at an altitude of up to 21,000 m, and had an effective range of 8000 m

18

SPRD-99 rocket-assisted take-off (RATO) bottles allowed MiG-21s to conduct 50 sorties from the taxyways at the badly-bombed Noi Bai airfield in 1972. This example is seen fitted to preserved MiG-21MF 5121, formerly of the 927th 'Lam Son' Fighter Regiment. The aircraft is displayed in Hanoi

NORTH VIETNAMESE STAMPS

Stamp 1

Hanoi claimed that USAF F-105D 61-0193, flown by Maj Ron Byrne of the 67th TFS/18th TFW, and shot down on 29 August 1965, was the 500th American aircraft to be destroyed over North Vietnam. After being hit by 37 mm flak, the ammunition in Maj Byrne's aircraft, which was based at Korat in Thailand, started to explode and flames began whipping back into his cockpit, forcing him to bail out over enemy territory. However, he had already managed to complete his mission, bombing the Yen Bai arsenal near the Red River. Shortly after hitting the ground, Byrne was captured and taken to the 'Hanoi Hilton', where he spent the next seven years in captivity.

Stamp 2

1Lt Donald W Bruch Jr's F-105D (62-4304, of the 333rd TFS/355th TFW, based at Takhli, Thailand) was claimed by the North Vietnamese to be the 1000th US aircraft brought down over North Vietnamese territory. One of a number of Thunderchiefs sortied on 29 April 1966 to attack the Thai Nguyen railway yard, the aircraft was about 12 miles north-east of Hanoi when it was struck by 85 mm flak. Lt Bruch was ordered to climb, and as he did the aircraft went out of control, entered a steep dive and crashed. No parachute was seen and no 'beepers' (emergency radio signals) were heard. Lt Bruch was listed as Killed in Action.

Stamp 3

1Lts Eugene T Meadows and Murray L Borden of the 480th TFS/366th TFW took off in F-4C 64-0654 from their base at Da Nang, South Vietnam, on 13 October 1966 on an armed reconnaissance mission over the north. Their aircraft was one in a flight of two Phantom IIs that was to make four passes over their target in Quang Binh province, about ten miles north of the eastern side of the Demilitarised Zone. On the fourth pass, Meadows and Borden failed to radio in, and the crew of the other aircraft saw a large explosion while preparing to make another run on the target. They circled the area, but heard no 'beepers'. Soon, however, a 'beeper' was picked up by SAR aircraft, but neither the crew nor the aircraft could be found. The men were listed as Missing in Action (MIA). Meadows' remains were identified on 21 November 1994, but Borden's have never been found. This aircraft was claimed by Hanoi as the 1500th US victim of the air war.

Stamp 4 (two stamps)

On 5 June 5 1967, Lt Cdr Collins H Haines (from VFP-63 Det L, embarked on the USS *Bon Homme Richard*) was piloting RF-8G BuNo 145614 on his 40th photographic reconnaissance mission, over a railway in Thanh Hoa province. As he passed about ten miles north-west of the city of Thanh Hoa, his aircraft was hit by 37/57 mm fire and it crashed. Upon ejection, his right leg flailed, his kneecap was broken, and he sustained other severe leg injuries. Haines, who the Vietnamese claimed to be the 2000th(!) US victim of the air war, was captured and held prisoner until Operation *Homecoming* in the spring of 1973.

Stamp 5

On 6 November 1967, Maj Robert Warren Hagerman flew F-105D 62-4286 of the 469th TFS/388th TFW, out of Korat, Thailand, on a combat mission against Hanoi's Gia Thuo storage dump. His aircraft was struck by a SAM while attacking the target, and Hagerman was listed as Killed in Action – his remains were eventually returned to the USA on 4 December 1985. According to the enemy, his was the 2500th US aircraft to come down over North Vietnamese territory.

Stamp 6

At that same time as the previous stamp was released, the Vietnamese also issued this rendition of a flaming B-52 diving earthward. Although marked with the 2500th kill titling, no specific details of the action that the stamp purports to represent have so far been located.

Stamp 7 (two stanps)

The North Vietnamese claimed that they chalked up their 3000th US victim on 24 June 1968 in the shape of Lt Nick Carpenter (pilot) and Lt(jg) Joseph S Mobley (bombardier-navigator) in A-6A Intruder BuNo 152949 of VA-35, embarked on the USS *Enterprise*. The aircraft was hit at low altitude by 37/57 mm flak near the city of Vinh. Both Lt Carpenter and Lt(jg) Mobley were listed as MIA, although Mobley's name was removed from the list in August 1969 when the Navy received word that he was a prisoner in the north. He was released in March 1973. Carpenter's remains were returned in January 1989. Ironically, neither of these 3000th victory stamps actually depict flak batteries, showing instead a MiG-17 downing what looks like an F-105, and an SA-2 pointing skyward towards an already doomed F-4.

Stamp 8 (two stamps)
Elderly militiamen and young women are honoured in these 3000th kill stamps. Both groups are diligently manning anti-aircraft guns.

Stamp 9 (two stamps)
RF-4C 68-0598 of the 14th TRS/432nd TRW, based at Udorn, in Thailand, was sent on a reconnaissance mission over the Dong Hoi truck park on 20 April 1972. Maj Ed Elias evaded one SAM, but not a second, and he was captured three days after he and his back-seater, 1Lt E S Clark, ejected from their burning Phantom II. WSO Clark was rescued, but Elias remained a PoW in the 'Hanoi Hilton' until he was released on 25 September 1973. The jet was the 3500th US aircraft downed, according to Hanoi. Note that only one stamp bears the date on which this shoot-down took place.

Stamp 10
On 17 October 1972, Capt James A Hockridge and 1Lt Allen U Graham were flying F-111A 67-0660 of the 429th TFS/474th TFW near the city of Cho Moi when they were shot down. Hanoi later released a photograph showing the ID tags of both men, and other military documents from the crash, as well as shots of the burned-out wreckage. 'Radio Hanoi' claimed that both crewmen died in the incident, and that this was the 4000th aircraft downed over North Vietnam. A later broadcast reported that some remains were recovered and buried along the Cau River. Both men were listed as MIA until their remains were returned by the Vietnamese on 30 September 1977.

Stamp 11
The second stamp released to mark the 3000th victory replaced the flak gunner with a shell-toting soldier, stood in front of a large-calibre anti-aircraft gun and an SA-2 missile.

Stamp 12
On 12 January 1973, Lt Victor T Kovaleski and his RIO Lt(jg) James Wise shot down a MiG-21. Two days later, while Kovaleski was flying with Ens D H Plautz over Thanh Hoa, his F-4B (BuNo 153068 of VF-161, embarked on the USS *Midway*) was hit by 85 mm AAA. He and the RIO ejected safely and were rescued. Lt Kovaleski had not only claimed the last victory against the VPAF, but he was also flying the last aircraft to be shot down over North Vietnam! The North Vietnamese stated that the VF-161 Phantom II was the 4181st US air victim of the war.

Stamp 13
The downing of the F-4B on 12 January 1973 was followed by the issuing of several stamps marked with the 4181st victory titling. This example shows a B-52 being shot down by a MiG-21.

Stamp 14
Another 4181st victory stamp, this time showing mine-laying B-52s being shot down by ships anchored in Hai Phong Harbour.

Stamp 15
The final 4181st kill stamp to be issued shows Vietnamese fishing boats trawling for wreckage along the northern coast of the Gulf of Tonkin. Note that these downed jets have all been identified by their various designations.

Stamps 16 to 21
These stamps illustrate the struggles of the Air Defence Forces/Vietnamese People's Air Force in 1967. The six-piece set, printed on 19 November 1967, shows an air defence unit (stamp 16), an anti-aircraft unit at a factory (stamp 17), a naval unit in battle (stamp 18), anti-aircraft batteries protecting a bridge (stamp 19), a dogfight between MiG-17s and US Navy F-4s in progress (stamp 20) and a captured American pilot (stamp 21). Two days prior to the release of these stamps, a group of 32 American aircraft (made up of F-105Ds and F-4C/Ds) was heading for Hanoi when it was attacked by three MiG-21s of the 921st Fighter Regiment. Vu Ngoc Dinh scored an F-105D kill with AAMs. A flight of MiG-17s was also involved, helping the MiG-21s down the F-4Cs over Ha Hoa. The rest of the aircraft turned for home after releasing their bombs.

MAPS

Map 1
30 April 1967
Three F-105Ds (59-1726, 61-0130 and 62-4447) of the 355th TFW were brought down by MiG-21s of the 921st Fighter Regiment

Map 2
18 May 1972
Two Phantom IIs 'fell' victim to MiG-17, -19 and -21 fighters on this day, although the USAF stated that only F-4D 66-7612 of the 421st TFS/366th TFW had been destroyed by MiG activity

INDEX

References to illustrations are shown in **bold**.
Colour Plates are prefixed 'pl.', Colour Section illustrations
'cs.' and Stamps 'st.', with page and caption locators in
brackets.

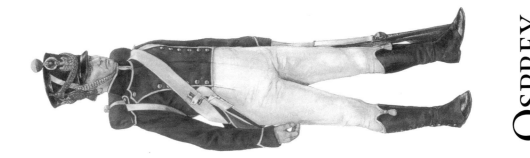

FIND OUT MORE ABOUT OSPREY

❑ Please send me a FREE trial issue
   of Osprey Military Journal

❑ Please send me the latest listing of Osprey's publications

❑ I would like to subscribe to Osprey's e-mail newsletter

Title/rank

Name

Address

Postcode/zip   state/country

e-mail

Which book did this card come from?

❑ I am interested in military history

My preferred period of military history is

❑ I am interested in military aviation

My preferred period of military aviation is

I am interested in (please tick all that apply)

❑ general history   ❑ militaria   ❑ model making
❑ wargaming   ❑ re-enactment

Please send to:

USA & Canada: Osprey Direct USA, c/o Motorbooks
International, P.O. Box 1, 729 Prospect Avenue, Osceola,
WI 54020

UK, Europe and rest of world:
Osprey Direct UK, P.O. Box 140, Wellingborough, Northants,
NN8 2FA, United Kingdom

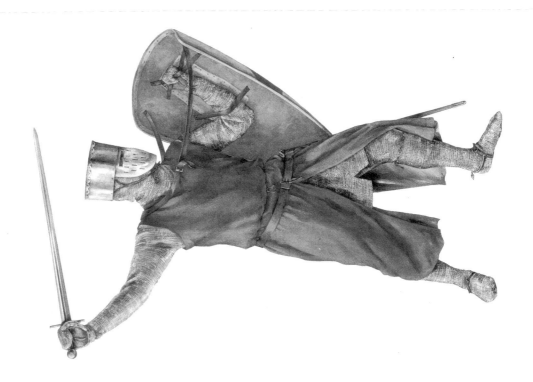

OSPREY
PUBLISHING

www.ospreypublishing.com

call our telephone hotline
for a free information pack

USA & Canada: 1-800-458-0454
UK, Europe and rest of world call:
+44 (0) 1933 443 863

Young Guardsman
Figure taken from *Warrior 22:
Imperial Guardsman 1799–1815*
Published by Osprey
Illustrated by Christa Hook

Knight, c.1190
Figure taken from *Warrior 1: Norman Knight 950 – 1204AD*
Published by Osprey
Illustrated by Christa Hook

POSTCARD